HER MAESTRO'S ECHO

HER MAESTRO'S ECHO

Pirandello and the Actress Who Conquered Broadway in One Evening

Pietro Frassica

t

Copyright © 2010 Troubador Publishing Ltd

Apart from any fair dealing for the purposes of research or private study, or criticism or review, as permitted under the Copyright, Designs and Patents Act 1988, this publication may only be reproduced, stored or transmitted, in any form or by any means, with the prior permission in writing of the publishers, or in the case of reprographic reproduction in accordance with the terms of licences issued by the Copyright Licensing Agency. Enquiries concerning reproduction outside those terms should be sent to the publishers.

Published by
Troubador Publishing Ltd
5 Weir Road
Kibworth, Leicester
Tel: (+44) 116 2792299

Email: books@troubador.co.uk
Web: www.troubador.co.uk

Series Editor
George Ferzoco
University of Bristol, UK

ISBN: 9781848763524

Typesetting: Troubador Publishing Ltd, Leicester, UK

For Tom,

Who dares swim against the current

TABLE OF CONTENTS

Preface	xi
My Marta	1
1. The Romance Novel of Life	**9**
Complex Collaborations	19
Frustrated Loves: "Ideal Interpreter of Pirandello's Theater"	29
A Rigid Program	42
2. Pirandellian Theater under Fascism	**53**
The Argentina Incident	55
"Unspeakable things are happening"	57
A Theatrical 'Rivalry' with Mussolini	61
Marta Appeals to Il Duce	66
Artists, Theater, and the State	71
3. The Hand that Turns the Crank	**75**
Silly Symphonies	85
Two Characters in Search of a Filmmaker	92
In the Artist's Studio	101
4. A Star is (Not Quite) Born	**113**
Mrs. Severance A. Millikin	121
Divorce	124
Impossible Loves	127
Marta's Bitter Homecoming	132
Pirandello Family Troubles	136
The d'Amico Dynasty	148
Epilogue: The Less than Affable Guardian	**155**
Works Cited	159

SIGLA

Quotations from the correspondence between Luigi Pirandello and Marta Abba are cited in the text with the abbreviations listed below.

P: Luigi Pirandello, *Pirandello's Love Letters to Marta Abba*, ed. and trans. Benito Ortolani (Princeton University Press, 1994).

L: Luigi Pirandello, *Lettere a Marta Abba*, ed. Benito Ortolani (Milan: Mondadori, 1994).

C: Marta Abba, *Caro Maestro,* ed. Pietro Frassica (Milan: Mursia, 1994).

U: Unpublished letters found in Firestone Library at Princeton University.

Translations from *Lettere a Marta Abba* and *Caro Maestro* are my own, as are citations from conversations with Marta Abba and other quotations cited from Italian sources, unless otherwise indicated. Quotations from the English translations in P have occasionally been modified based on comparison with the originals.

PREFACE

While Luigi Pirandello (1867-1936) is certainly among the most studied of 20th-century Italian authors, he remains mysterious and strangely distant, inviting ever more investigation and interpretation. His varied texts, literary (poetry, short stories, novels), theatrical, essays (philosophical, aesthetic, philological, interpretative), and personal (letters, confessions, memoirs), continue to provide a seemingly inexhaustible source for widely different readings by successive generations of readers.

Pirandello's literary career began when he moved to the University of Rome as a student, and then to Bonn, Germany, in 1891, completing his degree in Philology and staying on for another year as lecturer. During these years, Pirandello published several volumes of poetry. Along with a sort of post-romantic pessimism and illusions about first loves, they display a desire to represent the sheer variety of life's many dramas and portray the intellectual and moral malaise typical of the turn of the century, and indicate Pirandello's poetic interest in Dante, Goethe, Heine and Leopardi. In 1894 he published a collection of short stories entitled *Amori senza Amore* (*Love stories without love*); in the same year, he married Antonietta Portulano, the daughter of his father's business partner. To support this mentally ill wife as well as his children, Pirandello began supplementing his teaching salary with work as a private literature tutor and by publishing small works here and there; among these, his second novel, *The Late Mattia Pascal*, a work which had a strong influence on twentieth-century Italian narrative, was published between April and June 1904 as a serial in the journal *Nuova Antologia*, as well as a series of short story collections. In 1908, he published two volumes of essays, *Arte e scienza* [*Arts and Sciences*] and *On Humor*, which articulated the poetic and aesthetic principles of his narrative and theater. Because his short stories trace, almost photographically, small vignettes of life, Pirandello thought to translate these photographs into the medium of theater, a more effective mirror of real life. On December 9, 1910 his career as a playwright began: at the Teatro Metastasio in Rome, two of his one-act plays were performed – one, *The Vise*, written in 1898 and originally entitled *The Epilogue*, that was based on his short story "The Fear," the other, *Limes from Sicily*, adapted from a short story of the same name. Thereafter, he dedicated ever more energy to this new genre, and a strong sign of growing recognition of his dramatic skills came in Milan, on April 19, 1915, when Marco Praga's theater company presented his play *If Not So* at the Teatro Manzoni. For such a prestigious director to stage this new playwright's play was a great honor. Meanwhile, he continued to write novels: *Her Husband*, 1911; *The Old and the Young* 1913; *Action!* 1915 and, *One, none, and one hundred thousand*, 1926.

Amidst personal crises and sorrows stemming from his wife's illness and his sons' participation in the First World War, Pirandello's success in the theater grew as more and more of his works were performed by well-known actors. He wrote many plays in these years: in 1913, *The Doctor's Duty*; in 1916, *Think it over, Giacomino!* and *Liolà*; in 1917, *The Jar, Right you are (if you think you are)* and *The pleasure of honesty;* and in 1918, *This time it will be different* and *The Rules of the game*. By the end of the war and with the safe return of his sons, Pirandello had definitively moved into the forefront of modern theater both in Italy (*Grafted and Man, Beast and Virtue* in 1919; *All for the best, As Before: Better than Before and Mrs. Morli, One and Two* in 1920) and abroad, especially after the opening of *Six Characters in Search of an Author* in 1921.

But Pirandello's career as a playwright could be conflicted at times. Alongside enthusiastic supporters, both the public and critics were often hostile to his works, as they introduced controversial novelties in conflict with many conventional practices in the theater. Reactions after the 1921 performance of *Six Characters* in Rome were indicative of this conflict: public outcry against the play and its author was so vehement that Pirandello had to remain backstage and could only leave the theater by a backdoor after everyone else had left. In *Six Characters*, he had begun to portray on stage the uneasiness of representation, dramatizing tensions between the text, the characters, and their author. These metatheatrical developments, in many ways revolutionary, continued to occupy Pirandello for the rest of his career. In 1922, his *Henry IV* was performed, and *Each in his own way* in 1924. In 1923 Pirandello began to travel abroad, following and overseeing various productions of his plays and attending many performances in Paris, London, Prague, Krakow, Amsterdam, Warsaw, Barcelona, New York, Vienna, Berlin, Athens, Tokyo. In 1924, a "Pirandello Season" was produced on Broadway. Then, in 1925, he accepted the opportunity to found and direct the Teatro d'Arte di Roma, which sought to promote young and promising playwrights, a position which brought him even closer to the world and daily lives of actors, giving him a privileged glimpse into and understanding of the roles and experiences of actors. The Teatro d'Arte was also the magical place where Pirandello met Marta Abba, a young Milanese actress who would become the company's star actress and with whom the writer would develop an intense and affectionate relationship. With Marta Abba the female characters in Pirandello's plays become protagonists, capable of dominating the stage in their own right, giving dramatic expression to the conflict between life and form. One can see this total fusion between writer and actress in *Diana* and *Tuda* (1926), *The New Colony* (1928) and in *As You Desire Me* (1930), the play that fits Marta Abba probably better than any other work that Pirandello wrote for her. In the Hollywood film version of *As You Desire Me* made two years later, Marta Abba was replaced by a bigger name: Greta Garbo.

In 1924, after the assassination of the Socialist leader Giacomo Matteotti, Pirandello joined the Fascist Party, a common enough move of self-preservation for intellectuals in the confusion of the times, but by 1927, Pirandello began to question his decision. He considered moving elsewhere, and in the fall of 1928, he relocated to Germany. Though busy with many international duties his creative activity continued. In 1928-29, in Berlin, he wrote *Belonging to One or No One* and *Tonight we improvise*, performed in German at Koenigsberg in 1930, *Lazarus* (performed in 1929, first in England, then in Turin), and *Dream, But Maybe Not*. 1929 is also the year when Pirandello began working on *The Mountain Giants*, the play that would occupy him until the end of his life, ultimately remaining unfinished. His last few plays include *To Find Oneself* (1932), written for Marta Abba, *When You Are Somebody* (1933), *The Fable of the Changeling* (1934), and *One Doesn't Know How* (1935). All this literary activity brought him much honorific recognition, including his election to the Accademia d'Italia (1929), and most notably, on December 10, 1934, he received the Nobel Prize for Literature. On the same day two years later, Pirandello, ill with pneumonia, died at his house in Rome while working on *The Mountain Giants*.

To understand Pirandello, one must bear in mind that, in his eyes, human identity is the product of perception and circumstance. Like mirrors, people are reflections of the world around them. Pirandello's life and his art symbolize the struggle between one's true self and the self which society imposes. This is the main reason why Pirandello has been identified from the beginning of his career as an intellectual playwright, more interested in ideas than in people, more concerned with abstractions than with their applicability to particular situations. His characters are often attacked for being either puppets manipulated for his own ends or abstractions lacking flesh and blood. Pirandello's plays do explore such complex issues as the multiplicity of human personality, the relativity of truth, and the difficulty — if not impossibility — of establishing boundaries between reality and illusion. The focus, however, is usually on the characters' interactions with these concepts as they struggle to deal with the effects such ideas have on their lives. Ideas do not exist in a vacuum for Pirandello, and any attempt to discuss his philosophy at a remove from those characters, treating them as symbols or puppets and not as people, risks grave distortion of his work.

The theater was the perfect medium for Pirandello's artistic expression, for what better place to deal with illusion, pretense, and role-playing than where actors assume a role for an audience that accepts them as those

The Romance Novel of Life

characters and yet is also aware of their existence as actors? Pirandello realizes that a character's theatricality need not be unexamined or unconscious, but can be used by its possessor for certain ends. He uses the theater self-consciously in the same way, to examine itself and its relationship to life. Just as the masks and illusions of life need to be examined with the assistance of the humorist who probes beneath their surface, so too must the theater, both the mirror of human actions and the source of what it sometimes reflects, be examined as it is being used to communicate insights into the human activities it imitates. Thus, in the plays usually referred to as his theater trilogy — *Six Characters in Search of an Author*, *Each in His Own Way*, and *Tonight We Improvise* — Pirandello pushes theater into modernism by attempting to explore the theatrical process and its relationship to the world it mirrors. Although the three plays were not composed as a trilogy in the usual sense, with continuity of either chronology or plot and character, they form a unity because each is set in the theater and takes theatrical experience as its subject matter and its major metaphor for the author's vision of life.

All three of the theater trilogy plays break through the imaginary 'fourth wall' of realistic theater in an attempt to destroy the barrier between auditorium and stage. Although each play includes many common dramatic figures, the focus of each work is on one of the three essential components of the process. *Six Characters* emphasizes the subject matter, the characters whose script is dramatized onstage; *Each in His Own Way*, the audience that views the theatrical performance; and *Tonight We Improvise*, the actors who interpret the script and bring it to life for the audience. Despite this difference in perspective for each play, the trilogy as a whole becomes an examination of the relationship between theater and life, their interdependence and interpenetration. In particular, with *Six Characters*, still his best-known play, Pirandello made a sharp break with his previous work, initiating a revolutionary turn in theater. It opened the window between the stage and the audience and eliminated much of the familiar theatrical decor.

These are some of the reasons why Pirandello is considered one of the foremost innovators in 20th-century theater. George Bernard Shaw is said to have called the *Six Characters* the most original play ever written (*The Shavian*, Feb. 1964). More than eighty years after its first performance in 1921, the play's power to fascinate is undiminished.

In the author's last creative period, which began around 1928-29, Pirandello entrusts his tortured investigations of truth to myths as a last hope for coherence, even if illusory, in the face of the relentless fragmentation of forms. The rejection of the world of contingency, against which Pirandello had first reacted with irony and then with dramatic contempt, develops finally into a nostalgic aspiration to a mythic absolute, generating a new form of fabulous and surrealistic theater. Works from this time are suffused with autobiography, reflecting his love for Marta Abba and displaying a depth of emotional expression not found in his earlier work. His eight years of correspondence with Marta testify strongly to the many apprehensions and hopes wrapped up in his last drama, *The Mountain Giants*, meant as a testament to the power of fantasy and poetry, but also to the tragedy of art in a brutal modern world. For this reason, *The Mountain Giants* was a constant companion through the vicissitudes of the relationship between writer and actress. In a sense, then, the final Marta, the truest Marta, is Ilse (the incarnation of the ultimate sacrifice of self to art) in *The Mountain Giants*, a work that was, by its very nature, impossible to finish, perhaps for reasons above and beyond the death of the author.

MY MARTA

Paris, 10.2.1931

My Marta,
I wish you were inspired to write to me more often, because the need I always have of your letters, as of air to breathe, is at this moment greater than ever, and I'll tell you why. I do believe that I am composing my masterpiece, *The Mountain Giants*, with a fervor and a trepidation that I can't express. I feel I have climbed to heights where my voice finds unheard-of sounds.... It matters little if you will not perform this work, either because you think it is not for you or because you won't be able to do so for whatever reason. This is a secondary problem. What not only matters but is also absolutely necessary for me at this moment is to think that I'm writing for you. I wouldn't be able to write one more word should your divine, inspiring image abandon me for one instant. I follow this image of you, in the situations in which I have placed it, and little by little it finds for me the words and creates for me the scenes, and carries me ahead—suggesting, showing me what the other characters must say, what they must do in order to answer to its vagaries, to placate or increase its anxieties, to forge out of the contrasting characters the supreme harmony of the composition. Without being aware of it, from so far away, perhaps not even thinking a little bit about me, consumed by other thoughts, by other preoccupations, you are doing my work. Now I wonder what

would happen if you were more alive to me, alive as you were before, when you used to think more and care more for your Maestro, who without you thinking of him (I say at least you're thinking of him) cannot live any longer...

Write to me, make yourself heard; I have all my art in you; you are my art; without your breath it dies. You are creating, and you do not know it, with all the power of your art, with the tones of your inimitable voice, with the splendor of your eyes that find the look for every passion; you are creating with the ardor that has come to me from your mind, from your heart, from all your person, so that I might transfer it into the work that I am writing through you and that is not mine but yours: *your creation*. Continue helping me until the very end, my Marta; do not abandon me; consider that not only would I die, but also your work. It is not possible for you not to be, as true and sole author, in everything I am still doing. But I am the hand. The one who dictates inside is you; without you, my hand becomes a stone.

Yesterday I had a little fever and perhaps I have it today, too; I took some packets of Fevre, and I'm taking care of myself; but it's nothing; *I am working!* I don't need anything anymore when I work: I need only you. If I receive a letter from you today, I will immediately be well. I believe that even if I should die, if a letter arrived I would rise from the dead. I am so alone, so alone, my Marta...(P, pp. 172-4)

Between 1925 and 1936 Luigi Pirandello wrote to the actress Marta Abba some 552 letters, including the one above, which was written in February of 1931. The letters are a splendid record of the vicissitudes of their decade-long relationship, although this correspondence remained enveloped in mystery for more than half a century. The first letter was written in February 1925. Unlike later, deeply passionate letters, it is a brief, businesslike message. But with it Pirandello unwittingly initiated one of the most important correspondences of the twentieth century. The letter above, written by a man clearly possessed by an overwhelming passion for the woman to whom he writes, reveals desires and frustrations on several levels at once—a longing for connection, a need to express his heart's and mind's dependence on her, insecurities about whether his intense longing is requited. But who was Marta, the woman who by 1931 had become for Luigi Pirandello his art, his sole personal muse, whose inspiration he needed so desperately as he worked on his ultimately unfinished masterpiece, *The Mountain Giants*?

Toward the end of 1924 a group of young Italian writers founded a new theater company, the "Teatro d'Arte di Roma," entrusting its artistic direction to Luigi Pirandello. By that time the Sicilian-born author had established himself as a leading playwright, having gained international acclaim in 1921 with the controversial production of his play *Six Characters in Search of an Author*. Since that time Pirandello's celebrity had been on the rise in the European theater world, and on New York's Broadway as well, where theater producer Brock Pemberton staged an entire season of his plays, running between October 1923 and January 1924.

The next year, on the evening of April 4, in a small theater built on the basement level of Rome's Palazzo Odescalchi, the new company inaugurated its activities with a performance of Pirandello's *Our Lord of the Ship*. In another play later that season, *Our Goddess* by the young playwright Massimo Bontempelli, the director cast Marta Abba, an aspiring young actress from Milan who had first won acclaim for her performance in Chekhov's *The Seagull*. In a letter dated February 7, 1925 and sent to the Teatro Chiabrera in Savona where Marta Abba was performing, Bontempelli asked the young actress if she would take the lead role in his play and introduced her to Pirandello, who added this brief postscript to the letter: "Please learn *Nostra Dea*'s leading role with love and be assured that your performance will be backed by a *prestigious* staging, which will make easier all the changes from one *costume* to the *next*" (P, p. 4; emphasis in original). In the play, the changing moods of the female protagonist are indicated by changes in costume.

Following this perfunctory professional note, the entire later correspondence between Pirandello and Marta Abba constitutes an epistolary diary that reveals extraordinary tensions between public and private, between the professional and the personal realms. In subdued tones, Pirandello voices the problems and fears of the last years of his life, while his drama, thanks largely to the presence of Marta Abba, acquires new life. In 1984, in Milan, I had the good fortune to see and to read Pirandello's then unpublished letters. I met with Marta Abba and she reminisced with me about her life with the Maestro (as she always called him) and about the ups and downs of her own life after his death in 1936. Marta died in 1988, and Pirandello's letters to her were published in Italian in 1995, with a selection published in English in 1994, the same year as my edition of Marta's letters to Pirandello (*Caro Maestro...Lettere a Luigi Pirandello 1926-1936*). This book, then, is about Marta, her life with and without Pirandello; it is a montage of words, images, ideas, and feelings drawn from the letters and the long conversations that I had with Marta Abba. My reading of Pirandello's letters, in conjunction with Marta's letters and the accounts that the former actress gave me in person, has afforded me the opportunity to reconstruct their story out of the profiles, encounters, moods, opinions, enthusiasms, hopes, sighs, tears, and crises that characterized the last ten years of the great playwright's life.

Luigi Pirandello was nearing sixty when he met Marta Abba. She was twenty-four. That the author was attracted to and became infatuated with a woman so much younger is hardly surprising—such infatuations are common. But to understand the larger picture of how Marta impacted his life, Pirandello's circumstances, artistic development and character must, however briefly, be taken into account. Born in Sicily in 1867, Pirandello had always been a dreamer and a romantic. Instead of taking up his father's business of sulfur mining, he pursued a university education, studied literature and linguistics, and began to write and teach. As a young man he wrote poetry, lyrical verses of love and pathos, sweet endearing descriptions in traditional romantic modes. But he soon turned to short fiction and novels, and finally to drama, on which he began to focus his talents around 1915. His novel *The Late Mattia Pascal*, published in 1904, gave him his first real literary success, and thereafter he was a force to be reckoned with on the international art and literary scene.

Coming of age in the late nineteenth century, with its great second wave of remarkable technological innovations, Pirandello's artistic and personal sensibilities were formed in response and reaction to these profound cultural changes. Gas lights, electric lights, telegraphs, telephones, phonographs, cinema, radio, automobiles, airplanes, electrified and motorized engines of all shapes and sizes—like all others of his generation, Pirandello was a living witness to the advent of these marvels. He had to make sense of them and the world that they were so quickly and deeply transforming. Technology is therefore a constant theme in Pirandello's literary productions, reflecting in many ways the author's own personal engagement with the technological revolution that gave birth both to European-American cultural modernity and to the large-scale bureaucratic modern state. Pirandello witnessed the rise of cinemas and the rise of Fascism in Italy—arguably not unrelated developments. Indeed, we get the sense from Pirandello's cultural pronouncements on new technologies that he was not entirely at ease with machines, and that at heart he retained something of that skeptical suspicion with which so many people greet cultural changes, whether moral or technical, that arise in the course of their lives.

When he met Marta, Pirandello's own family life was far from idyllic. In 1894 he had married Antonietta Portulano, the daughter of one of his father's business associates. It was an arranged marriage, and he did not know her well before they wed. Antonietta, a beautiful girl from the bourgeoisie of Agrigento, brought with her a large dowry that was invested in the sulfur mine of Pirandello's father in exchange for a monthly disbursement. Before their marriage the young writer tried to inform his fiancée of his disposition and what to expect of him, especially with respect to his creative endeavors—he wanted her to understand that he would need her support during those times of sadness and uneasiness that Art can sometimes bring. However, one gets the sense that in her mind she always had the feeling that she could not satisfy her husband's expectations. Her one consolation was the generous dowry, which compensated in some measure for other deficiencies she felt responsible for.

The couple had three children, a girl and two boys, but Antonietta's health was not good, and she suffered a nervous breakdown after the birth of their son Fausto in 1899. This crisis seemed to resolve itself shortly thereafter without leaving any permanent effects on Antonietta, but her physical and emotional difficulties were aggravated in 1904 by the sudden news from Sicily that the Pirandello sulfur business had been destroyed by flooding in the mines—destroying along with it her dowry, which had so prominent a place in her ever-fragile sense of purpose in the family. She became obsessive, paranoid, and increasingly difficult to live with. She exhibited a strange jealousy, stemming from Pirandello's position at an all-female university. This jealousy extended to the family's maids, all of whom Antonietta fired out of suspicion that they were rivals for Luigi's affections, and even to their daughter, Lietta, who in turn was very disturbed by her mother's behavior and on at least one occasion attempted suicide. Her sons' participation in the First World War only worsened Antonietta's condition, and in 1918, Lietta, no longer able to cope with it, fled Rome and stayed with her aunt and uncle in Florence; the next year Pirandello made the desperate decision to commit his wife to the care of an institution.

His wife's long years of torment and illness profoundly influenced Pirandello's work. Madness and alienation pervade his writing, and the female characters in works before he met Marta are often tormented, obsessive, and suicidally passive victims of life. After he met Marta, on the other hand, his female characters become strong, outspoken and active. The difference is night and day; it reflects the torments Pirandello witnessed and suffered with his wife, and the fresh inspiration he received when Marta suddenly entered his life. Thus the story of Marta Abba is the integral and climactic last chapter in the life and career of one of the most influential figures in modern European theater.

But Marta's own story also deserves to be told in its own right. After all, she lived for fifty years after her Maestro died, although the shadow of his influence never quite lifted from her life. Everything she did and suffered, her circumstances and difficulties, were constantly affected by the playwright's problematic legacy. Not least, she had to engage in acrimonious legal struggles with his family over rights to his plays. This book, then, is an attempt to sketch out the story of this modern romance, between an author and an actress, between an artist and his collaborating muse, between an older man and younger woman. Much has been written about Pirandello, the great artist and grandiose personality; Marta's side of the story, on the other hand, has never adequately been told, and on certain points I feel a sense of duty to her to give her a fair hearing. In addition, the story touches on areas that will perhaps be of broad and general appeal: some intriguing behind-the-scenes vignettes in the early history of filmmaking, including Pirandello's suspicions of Walt Disney; Marta's meeting with Mussolini, a fan of hers, and her candid impressions of him; Marta's marriage of convenience into the prominent Ohio family of the Millikins; glimpses of an Italian media dynasty and its heavy-handed influence on the arts in general, and on Pirandello's afterlife and Marta's career in particular.

In the letters exchanged by Pirandello and Marta Abba, we see a series of memories and immediate impressions filing past before our eyes: the Fascist atmosphere of Rome; Milan at the end of the twenties and into the thirties; a lively and stimulating Berlin; an elegant and cosmopolitan Paris; and theatrical activities in Buenos Aires, London, and New York in the thirties. Alternating between expressions of personal thoughts, fears, and preoccupations, and long descriptions of their feverish labors, their hopes for fruitful business engagements, the story that evolves in the correspondence puts private and everyday life within the context of the age and its history. The letters, so full of inventiveness, alternate the tragic and the comic, the poetic and humorous, but the tone is always determined by love, which is the sole meaning of everything, the fundamental reason behind every initiative and every moment of reflection, and which becomes the reason for living and even a substitute for life itself.

It is a story that spans a century, from Luigi Pirandello's formative early literary career in the late nineteenth century to Marta Abba's bequest of her collected correspondence to Princeton University Library in the 1980s. But its constant center of gravity is the eleven-year period between 1925 and 1936, when Pirandello's life, nearing its end, was changed forever by his encounter with Marta Abba, and when Marta's life, still in its formative stages, was stamped indelibly with the playwright's distinctive genius. It is here—with the romance of their meeting and a decade of intensifying collaboration—that the story begins.

Chapter I

THE ROMANCE NOVEL OF LIFE

Taken together, Pirandello's letters to Marta Abba read, almost intentionally, like a romance novel, and in many respects they are akin to his novels, short stories and plays. But unlike his published works, the letters show a much more direct, albeit repressed, personal involvement. Each time the two part ways he feels an immediate, nagging regret about what might have been: "After Your departure on that devil of a night train that seemed to me to be a brutally violent act of rape on you, and on me, from which I was able to free myself only with difficulty, you can imagine what my thoughts were" (Rome, September 21, 1928; L, p. 47). After another departure he writes: "You are still traveling, and still I follow you with my thoughts, as I've been doing since the first moment the train departed. How I was feeling—you can imagine" (Berlin, 14 March 1929; P, p. 30). But the young actress' reticent responses produced an all-consuming sense of insecurity:

> I was so happy to see your previous letters signed 'Marta'—the last one, from today, was on the contrary signed 'Marta Abba' and was cold, icy cold.
>
> Please do not interpret this remark as a reproach. If you could only realize how much good your letters do me and how I have blessed them all! (Nettuno [Rome], 12 July 1928; P, p. 20)

Again, the following spring, he longs for her return:

> Let's hope that fate, at least one more time before I close my eyes forever, might wish to be kind to me and lead you back to

me, Marta, so that I may get back one reason for living, which right now is completely lacking . . . you must give me the strength to endure. Only you can give it to me.

I'll keep following you with my thoughts as you travel until 7:45. And from 8:00 on I will picture you at home. I see it as if I were there.

And you, do you see me? (Berlin, 14 March 1929; P, p. 31)

Her very absence breeds new hope for future encounters, while his work becomes a prison in which he locks himself, serving two purposes, each of which is now bound up with Marta. On the one hand, his work and the letters he writes to her give him a means of escape, protecting him from the need to face an actual relationship with a woman. On the other hand, they reinforce his romantic notion that writing about a relationship is his only reason for existing:

It is truly written that salvation, in moments of the worst tempest, must come from work, to which I desperately cling. Work, work . . . (Rome, 17 July 1926; P, p. 9)

And I have been writing in order not to go mad. (Rome, 21 July 1926; P, p. 13)

Living for me means to work, to create; when I'm not able to do so any longer, it's a hundred times better for me to die. (Rome, 27 October 1935; P, p. 301)

The letters thus became an integral part of the overall fabric of Pirandello's writing (which had always been, in turn, a complete substitute for life), and were grafted directly onto the plays the author was currently working on. Indeed, lines of plays are often incorporated into his letters to Marta. More strikingly, just as frequently we find sentences in the plays that have been taken from *her* letters to him, which she tends to write in a Pirandellian style.

Given the nature of fiction, any romance novel is a substitute, even a negation, of actual love, and this is no less true of Pirandello's epistolary novel involving Marta. For many reasons, a romantic relationship with Marta was something he prevented himself, and was prevented by her and other external circumstances, from realizing, and thus his letters are a substitute for a more substantial flesh and blood relationship. Consider, for instance, his letter of August 25, 1926 (L, pp. 25-6), when Pirandello has an appointment with Marta in Genoa. He is anxious because he wants to arrive before her so he can welcome her when she arrives at the station. Thus he asks her to let him know by telegram the exact time of her arrival, admitting that he is willing to leave Rome a day earlier just to make sure he is there to meet her: "I don't want you to arrive before me and us to have to go looking for each other, without finding each other." Is this his real fear, we may wonder, or is he expressing an unconscious desire, which is channeled into the mundane practicalities of meeting up at a train station?

His words often employ the most formulaic clichés of love letters, with a persistent recourse to the "turmoils of the heart", which, by his own account, he meditates upon in the sleepless silence of the night: "So many nights I cannot sleep at all. *And I have been writing* in order not to go mad" [Rome, August 21, 1926, P, p. 13; original emphasis). After all, the writer has no real need to work his letters into literature, since he is already, by trade, completely immersed in it. Moreover, Pirandello had never been one of those writers who 'write beautifully,' and did not allow himself to be seduced by flowery language or aesthetics (much less by the baroque aesthetic then in vogue—that of Gabriele d'Annunzio, for example). To say that the correspondence is a romance novel is by no means to imply that it is a creation arising *out of* amorous experience. Rather, it involves the replacement of that experience by the written word. We are faced with a certain impotence, not in writing about what he feels inside (he does in fact write), but more in an inability to make love possible in a real-life relationship: "I wish I knew music to express, without being understood by anyone, not even by you, all this tumult of life that swells my soul and my heart. Nobody will ever know it, dear Marta, even if my heart should explode because of it" (Nettuno [Rome], 8 July 1928; P, p. 20).

In these letters Pirandello reflects his own multifaceted self more than he actually communicates, as if he is trying to avoid the unbearable reality of the 'other' through a play of mirrors that is very much in accord with his genius. But this constant mirroring also serves his purposes very well. Take, for instance, the little picture of her that she gives him when she leaves Germany: "I look at your picture smiling at me, as if to give me courage. Then I think that this is not true; that this image smiles for itself, and not for me; and then this smile, which is so beautiful, so full of noble grace, turns cruel to me, and my glance reproaches it, while my heart delights in it" (Berlin, March 14, 1929; P, p. 31). Like anyone in love, he watches over Marta even when he is far away and always wants to protect her. He has her interests in mind so much that he insists on an identity of their interests and even a union, through work interests, of their very selves:

> Please start thinking right now, *seriously*, about YOUR company, which you'll have next September. Think of the plays you'd like to stage—not mine, nothing mine: we'll talk about this point together, maybe we'll discuss it. In September you must have *your* company. Leave to me all the worries for the material realization of it. You, and *only you*, will be in charge. You do not need anyone else but me, and saying me is the same as saying *yourself*, because I am nothing else but *you*; I cannot consider myself otherwise, and you too should not consider yourself otherwise. *I*, for *us*, means *you*. . . Marta must think of nothing but *her* repertory, her interpretations, her company, and her dresses, not to pay for them, but for the joy of wearing them and adapting them to the roles she plays. Marta must not weep, Marta must not despair, Marta must always think that for her there is always *Her Luigi*. (Berlin, March 28, 1929; P, pp. 48-9; original emphasis).

We should note that despite Pirandello's promise to take care of "all the worries" regarding the "material realization" of Marta's company, it was Marta's father, not Pirandello, who a few months later provided financial backing to found the new company. He was a businessman who owned several jewelry and trinket shops in downtown Milan, the kind of store quite common in Italy at the time where women could find all sorts of jewelry, knick-knacks and curios, both inexpensive and quite valuable. In fact, later in life Marta still possessed several pieces from her father's collection that she was very proud of, including a lovely white-gold pin, adorned with rubies and emeralds, which her father had purchased from a Russian aristocrat after the Bolshevik revolution in 1917.

At other times, the letters, always full of affection for the writer's own preoccupations, hopes, and constant scrutiny of the state of his soul, oscillate between amorous conversation and the didactic instructions of master to student, a feature basic to the archetypal epistolary romance, such as the famous one between Abelard and Heloise. There are endless questions about her activities, plans, and preparations: "I am dying to know what you are doing, what you think, what you are going to do, what you feel. . . . Did you go to the theater? How do you spend your evenings? Do you plan to go, as you were saying, to the Riviera, to San Remo? Will you go there alone? What hopes do you have for the coming year? Are you preparing yourself? Are you reading something? Did you go to see [...] the *Three Sisters* by Chekhov" (Berlin, March 22, 1929; P, pp. 39-40). And again, a few weeks before he died, without pausing to give her any advice or to play the role of the old master: "I am happy about what you tell me about Your triumph in New York. It is the only thing that comforts me and helps me to bear this dismal life without You" (Rome, November 14, 1936; L, p. 1382). Sometimes he even converts their real relationship into a self-reflexive act, and turns her reticent confidences into evidence of requited love. For instance, Pirandello interprets the physical pains Marta describes in her letters as symptoms of a depression that is primarily erotic. Such depression had always been the true nourishment of *his* entire existence, and it is not without shivers of delight that he considers the 'cures' that he could furnish for these pains:

> But you are also ALL, Marta mia. And believe me, all you are suffering—your tiredness, your aches, all the pains that seem to be coming from the body but are not, pains of which no physician will ever find the cause—have on the contrary their root in this: that they are Life, all the Life that is in you, all the possibilities of being that are in you and live in you, without your even realizing it. They wear you out, distress you, depress you, exasperate you, continuously and vehemently taking your spirit by storm, or trying to forcibly remove the blocks of your conscience—perhaps too narrow and bourgeois—inside which you keep yourself bottled up. Meanwhile your will remains inert and does not rise up either to defend your body from these violent winds of the spirit which so many times I see flashing through your astonished and engrossed eyes, or to persuade your conscience to release those brakes and satisfy the bursting demands of both your spirit and your flesh. I could be a great physician for you, my Marta. But it would be necessary that you be entrusted to my care alone (Nettuno [Rome], July 13, 1928; P, p. 21).

Marta's actual agency in any of these exchanges is further eclipsed by the playwright's overactive fantasy. He is far too accustomed to imagining (theatrical) actions and reactions not to know what the young woman is doing in his absence, especially since that woman is *his* own actress, who behaves and speaks with the gestures and words he has devised for her:

> I imagined you in bed, and then when you got up, and then . . . then suppositions about maybe she is doing this, maybe she is doing that. I am almost positive that you did not go out in the morning. You probably went out in the afternoon, but where to? My trouble is this, that my imagination, which still sees you in all the hours of the day, does not know where to follow you . . . (Berlin, March 16, 1929; P, p. 35).

But the terrible thing is that Marta both is *and* represents the other, and as such she is entirely foreign and unknown. This aspect of his internal frustration emerges especially when the writer seems to be approaching the stage of the disillusioned lover since, as often happens, when love fastens upon its object, that object tends to vanish:

> …you did not want me anymore and you went away. If I were still in your heart, you would always have *me* — and *only me* you should have not reproached for wanting to deny you comfort. *The fact is that you do not keep me in your heart anymore.* This is for me the dreadful truth. Otherwise you would have not gone away. That is why you feel alone. You find yourself faced with a *useless* life because of this. You think that (God forbid!) in dying you would bring grief *only to your family*. To me, no! I therefore do not exist at all anymore for you. You show it with facts, you say it with words . . . (Berlin, Easter day, 1929; P, p. 55; original emphasis).

Above all, in reading the letters we develop a strong desire to know whether *Luigi*, as he sometimes signed his letters ("I cast away *Pirandello*, which was an unbearable weight to me as I wrote to you, but if you wish, I will go back to it" [Berlin, 21 March 1929; L, p. 80]), was truly in the heart of *his* Marta. Letter writing, we must remember, is necessarily an activity conducted in the *absence* of the other person. When the two are together we are of course not privy to their communications. But neither does their correspondence provide a solid answer as to whether he was ever in her heart. How could it, after all, since this is the crux of his own anxieties, which prompt him to cast out endless passionate overtures, desperately expecting her to respond in kind. But Marta's letters to him are no more illuminating, since she always maintains a friendly and conversational tone, and never makes reference to the place he thinks he occupies in her heart. She expresses respect for her mentor and does not hesitate to seek his advice. Occasionally she even offers him advice. But not only does she give no sign of reciprocating his passion for her, she even scolds him for being too passionate, and for his accusations, arising out of jealous frustration, that she does not write him often enough.

When she feels investigated and accused, her tone, which is usually pleasant, becomes defensive, and she feels inclined to fill up the page with details that will not arouse his suspicion. But then Pirandello, who discerns that Marta is intentionally holding back some news, protests, accusing her of writing trivialities. She then repeats that:

> with everything I have to do and keep track of, (for instance, I just got through a long argument over a matinee we were to do under contract and which fell through because of papa's and Rissone's [manager of the Marta Abba Theater Company] lack of firmness) and I couldn't begin to say how many of these discussions, not to say quarrels, I had, this was going on in Naples, and meanwhile you were telling me my letters were vacuous, worse than vacuous, and I don't know how I can still have the breath to speak to you!" (Messina, April 12, 1930; C, p. 78)

We may well wonder what Pirandello really means when he says that "you do not keep me in your heart anymore." Does it mean that Marta was once in love with the Maestro who is constantly thinking of her? Or is it only that the love he views as absolute has so dazzled him that he cannot help but project onto Marta an image of himself burning with desire, and thereby he convinces himself that she too is, or once was, inflamed by the same ardent love? Traces of this bedazzlement, glimpsed in an insistent and evocative metaphor of light (a rhetorical system that evokes the sublimity of medieval poetry), can be found in the following quotation, in which the end of the hoped-for love does not refer simply to the end of a relationship, but rather to the fading of the vital potential the woman embodies, giving the illusion of remaining alive as long as her presence sustains it. We move, therefore, from love as a possibility created in the absolute, to be worshipped without words in its luminous essence, to love as disappointment and despair, kept alive *in absentia* through mere words that describe the impossibility of its realization:

> I would have caught more than an airplane if you—instead of recalling me to Italy for the elections to the Academy [of Italy, created in 1929 by Mussolini, with Pirandello as a founding inductee]—would have called me back to stay again near you. Because now, after three years of living close by you, I feel that without you, although I try very hard to resist, I am dying. I am dying because I no longer know what to do with my life; in this horrible loneliness there is no more sense for me in living—neither value nor purpose. The meaning, the value, the purpose of my life all were you—in hearing the sound of your voice close to me, in seeing the heaven of your eyes and the light of your glance—the light that was brightening my spirit. Now everything is dead and extinguished, inside me and around me. This is the terrible truth. There is no point in my making it known to you; but it is so. It is my fault, because I allowed myself to be caught up again by life, when I shouldn't have. Now it is no longer possible for me to feel abandoned by it. The more the days go by, the more my anguish and despair grow; and I don't know what will happen to me tomorrow..." (Berlin, March 20, 1929; P, pp. 37-8).

The deeply dramatic tone of most of his letters becomes understandable, on one level, when we realize that Pirandello is often engaging in a sort of dialogue with his (sometimes imaginary) antagonist, without the reader—in this case Marta—realizing it. As an actor who never forgets, even in 'real' life, that he is acting a part, so Pirandello is unable to put aside completely his role as the protagonist in the correspondence, or that freedom of fantasy and role-playing that the fictional space of writing allows him. Even in his reticence, and despite his absolute control of information, he reveals a certain desire to negate the immediate pleasure of reading. Like anybody who is an avid writer of letters, he is writing to, and for, himself—hence the narcissistic tendency that does not let him resist the voluptuous pleasure of self-exhibition. This occurs even when his letters, by exposing all the conflicting movements of his mind, project the image of a man afflicted by the pangs of love, and revealing, perhaps not entirely consciously, the subtle tricks and manipulations of his art.

Tracing the evolution of the Pirandello-Abba relationship in his letters is like watching a game that is at times naive, at other times tinged with cruelty. The obstinate desire he reveals, at first sight, to be distant and alone, might seem on closer inspection to be a renunciation of the relationship that in many ways appears to be his only and ultimate reason for living. In reality it is the only option allowed to him—that he allows himself—because in this way he can write *her* and write *it*. That is, he can make her his own in a manner that is at once omnipotent and impotent, because it is possible only through writing. In order to exist, love must become a romance novel, passing from intolerable reality to the unrealizable sublimity of truth. And thus the love story recounted (and imagined) in the correspondence unfolds as a progressive supplementing of vital matter (unrealizable eros) with the imperishable materials of art, just as in the climax of *Find Oneself*, a play he wrote for Marta in 1932. When the love of the play's protagonist, Donata Genzi, for Eli fails, and she realizes the impossibility of ever finding true intimacy, in an exhortation to poetry, to pure creativity possible only through the living sacrifice of the creator, she cries out at last: "And this is true . . . And it is not true . . . True is only that which needs to create itself, create! And only then can one find oneself" (*Find Oneself*, end of Act 3).

On the other hand, writing to Marta means not only speaking about himself and the desire to be close to her, but also discussing his work, and especially comparing his female characters with Marta. He felt she possessed special insights that made her both the ideal interpreter and the ideal performer of his work, and it was expressly for her that he wrote most of the plays in the last decade of his life. His letters then become the author's diary, closely intertwined with his shifting daily emotions and an essential part of them, since the writer entangles 'his' actress in an intense working relationship, talking about the characters he is writing for her, asking her advice, requesting her participation and active collaboration. Writing to her regularly, struggling with his real passion for her, needing both her presence and absence as a true collaborator and as an erotic, frustrating muse, his habit of correspondence becomes a sort of first-level filter through which his intense experiences and emotions are transmuted to his imagination. In this way love and art are completely interwoven and end up creating together the enchanted castle of his writing.

Complex Collaborations

To understand the complex role Marta played in Pirandello's work from the epiphany-like moment she entered his life, we need only recall the description of Tuda/Marta at her first appearance in the play *Diana and Tuda*: "She is very young and astonishingly beautiful. Her hair is tawny, wavy, and done up in the classical style of ancient Greece. Her mouth has a sort of forlorn expression, as if life usually makes her scornful and bitter: but, by laughing, she suddenly displays a brilliant gracefulness, which lights up and breathes life into each and every thing." That is Marta!

From the day the playwright encountered the actress, he was taken with her as a personality for whom and with whom he could write dramas. In other words, he began to make her his actress, coauthor, and ideal critic all at once. In August 1926, for instance, after completing *Their Wives' Girl-Friend* (*L'amica delle mogli*), Pirandello writes to Marta that he cannot wait to have her read the play so that he can have her reaction. As it happened, one day that summer while the two of them were together in Livorno, Marta read *Diana and Tuda* in a hotel room whose balcony faced the sea. At this point Pirandello states that, unlike Tuda, Marta—which just happens to be the name of the main character of *Their Wives' Girl-Friend*—is like no other woman in the world. He has thus not only created a character completely his own, but also succeeded in eliminating any distinction between actress and character. This is part of the larger process, so prevalent and even transparent in the correspondence, of conflating the person of the author, the person of the actress, and the characters in his plays.

As soon as he learned Marta's opinion, which was not entirely positive, Pirandello immediately revised his work. Then, while Marta was on vacation in Salsomaggiore with her mother and her sister Cele, he let her know that he had corrected the third act of the play on the basis of her observations. Having made the revisions, he hoped to have her definitive approval, and he reiterated his conviction that only her assistance and contribution could bring his work to perfection: "You know," he writes, "how highly I esteem your intelligence and sensitivity in matters of art. I have no doubt that you see better than I do in my things" (August 15, 1926; U).

It is not only concerning theatrical matters that the author solicits the actress' opinion; he also asks her about novels he has already published. In the same letter from August of 1926, when he finds out that she has read *The Late Mattia Pascal* and *The Outcast*, Pirandello tells Marta that he is pleased and would like to know, when they next meet, how "Marta will talk about Marta." Marta Ajala was the name of the protagonist in *The Outcast*, a novel Pirandello had first published in 1893 as *Marta Ajala*, but had reissued in 1901 under the new title, the very same year Marta Abba was born! It was precisely this sort of 'coincidence,' linking the earlier fictional Marta with the real Marta of his present life, that tended to feed Pirandello's uncanny sense that his creative works had a prophetic tendency—that through his writings he was somehow predicting, and even shaping, his future life.

Marta's talents and intuitive power as an actress, coupled with her natural ability to immerse herself in Pirandellian characters, even those not expressly written for her, allowed her to be perfectly attuned to the author's ideas. Thus Pirandello found in her the ideal person to express the spirit of total sacrifice that his work required: the sacrifice of the individual for the sake of the character as part of the process of substituting the sublimity of art for the banality of life and eros. The first play he wrote 'for her,' *Diana and Tuda*, is telling in this respect. Its female protagonist, Tuda, is a model who poses for a sculptor while he slowly, painstakingly sculpts a statue of the goddess Diana in her image. It is a perfect, which is not to say transparent, allegory of artistic creation—of transmuting the flesh and blood embodiment of forms into the more enduring and idealized images of beauty in art. But the process of transformation leaves Tuda the woman feeling empty and exhausted, as though her very spirit has been captured and transferred through the sculptor's art into the statue of Diana. Her 'labor' as a model has turned out to be a costly self-sacrifice, an unexpected and intense collaboration with the more 'active' artistic role of the sculptor.

A closer look at the play's character dynamics reveals much about Pirandello's psychological turmoil as he works through the drama's thematic scenarios with Marta in his mind. A model of perfect beauty, Tuda poses for Sirio Dossi, a wealthy young sculptor who has dedicated himself to art in order to create one work, a statue of Diana. After finishing the sculpture and fulfilling his dream, Dossi decides to kill himself. Tuda is therefore indispensable for the work he is creating. The idea that Tuda could pose for other artists, allowing her beauty and the perfect harmony of her form to be interpreted differently by others, disturbs him profoundly, and drives him toward a kind of obsession. Tuda reminds him that if he wants a model all to himself, he should marry her. He accepts the proposal and marries her, not because she is a flesh-and-blood woman, but because in her lies the essence of his work of art. He already has a relationship with Sara Mendel; he will give Tuda his name and his wealth in exchange for her faithfulness as a model, and not necessarily for her faithfulness as a wife. Indeed, Sirio does not consider Tuda either as a wife or as a living being. What he loves in her are those forms that allow him to sculpt his Diana. After the completion of the statue, Tuda will have fulfilled her function. Herein springs her inner torment, as she feels increasingly deprived as the statue takes on a more definite shape. But her soul, her body, her own feelings and her existence are of no importance to the sculptor, who crystallizes these forms in his statue, which embodies merely the cold and lifeless spoils of Tuda herself. At this point, the model falls in love with the sculptor, but his insulting indifference causes her to provoke him with the only betrayal open to her: posing for another artist.

Tuda thus becomes a symbol of ideal feminine beauty and, as she grows more and more attached to the role she has been given, becomes not only Sirio's inspiration, but also his guide in the conceptualization of his work. On the other hand, Tuda has unwittingly been made a prisoner in her own game, which will keep her from rebelling and expressing herself freely in other ways.

Between the literal and the symbolic, the tragedy comes to its fatal conclusion. It is an old sculptor named Giuncano, also hopelessly in love with Tuda, who will resolve all the conflicts. When the statue is finished, Tuda is transformed. It is as if she were withering away after having given so much of her own beauty to the form of the statue, and she therefore feels great resentment and bitterness toward it. Later she will throw herself in desperation against the statue, screaming, "And I should be in there!" To protect his precious work Sirio lunges between the statue and Tuda. But Giuncano intervenes like a wild beast, and in order to defend Tuda he grabs Sirio by the throat, drags him violently to the floor and leaves him there dead.

Written for Marta, with her constantly in Pirandello's thoughts, what tortured labyrinths of desire and resistance, of repression and sublimation this play reveals! Despite *Diana and Tuda*'s warm reception after its first performance, it is certainly Pirandello's least-performed play, perhaps because the conflict between life and art is present in an overly compact form. Only later will it be developed in a more probing and less condensed fashion. *Diana and Tuda* should be seen as containing, in embryonic form, the themes Pirandello will develop in later plays through other female characters who are also conceived for Marta, and who personify the conflict between being and appearance.

While working on the third act of *Their Wives' Girl-Friend*, Pirandello writes to Marta that "the new play was born from you and for you. And so it is really yours. Do you remember the first time we spoke about it together? And now, a few days later, it is finished" (Rome, August 21, 1926; P, p. 13). In the letters there is no shortage of ideas for future plays. The author will first announce an idea in a letter, and then we can trace its progress in subsequent letters over a period of a few weeks, at the end of which the work is finished. Sometimes, however, as with *The Mountain Giants*, the ideas remain suspended among other works yet to be realized:

> "The same applies for *The Mountain Giants*—I find myself always thinking about it. I am strongly tempted to start writing this other myth of mine, the third and the last—but I must overcome this temptation and go for something practical. I can envision its scenes, each one more beautiful than the next; I see its characters, all of them, one by one; I caress them with my fantasy; last night, a sleepless night, the first scene was done from the beginning to the end; God knows what an effort I had to make this morning, when I got up, to leave it there and open instead the file where there are already 24 typewritten pages of *Either of One or No one*" (Berlin, April 8, 1929; P, p. 65).

And yet a year later Pirandello is still ruminating on his unfinished masterpiece:

> I started again to write with so much fervor! *The Mountain Giants*, my Marta, will be a truly gigantic work. I have thought things . . . things. . . . But I don't know how they can be produced, I don't say in Italy, but even here. . . . Great things! Prodigious! I took the story of *Il figlio cambiato* and I transformed it splendidly to serve as drama: the drama that the heroic countess is carrying around, at the price of her life. The transformation has come out so well that also this time, as for *As you desire me*, I must force myself to overcome the temptation to make out of it a work by itself: it would come

out magnificent! I'll talk to you about it tomorrow. But I have thought and I am thinking of many other things. It would be a real pity if I should die right at this moment! But I'll not die, I'll not die, knock on wood! (Berlin, April 17, 1930; P, p. 124).

In a letter to Marta two years earlier, he had also described the screenplay based on *Six Characters in Search of an Author* as something belonging only to them (I will discuss the peculiarities of this screenplay in the next chapter):

"I have it by now almost all completed in my mind. As soon as we're together, in Genoa, I'll explain it to you for your approval and, who knows, maybe also your collaboration, because I would like this work to be in everything and for everything OURS, born of THE TWO OF US, one thing and OURS. You'll see how many ideas I have thought about, and how well it will come out, and everything will be clear, extraordinarily powerful on the levels of fantasy and drama!" (Nettuno [Rome], July 13, 1928; P, pp. 21-2).

In the artistic collaboration between Pirandello and Marta Abba there is a constant exchange of ideas and suggestions, both for immediate and for long-term projects. The actress' participation extends not only to the plays that Pirandello is writing but also to practical matters. Her organizational skills, along with her father's financial help, allowed her to establish in 1929 her own theater company, which toured Italy for several seasons. The letters written by both parties reveal common problems of the theatrical world: selecting the repertoire, casting, financial difficulties and their possible solutions, struggling to get into the most prestigious theaters, disputes with theater managers and agents, inevitable jealousies, disagreements with critics and the press, and disappointments over unrealized projects. Letters Pirandello wrote while he was abroad, for example, show his attempts to create suitable conditions for himself and Marta to launch their careers outside Italy. Besides letters he sent from

Berlin, London, and Paris, those he sent from the United States also assume a particular importance. In these he describes, with a plethora of detail, the impact that America made on him, including his plans for Marta's success on Broadway and in Hollywood. At every point the actress is consulted, or at least used as a sounding-board, for his possible solutions, and she, for her part, responds with characteristic level-headedness to his ideas. Moreover, with regard to the actual writing of plays, Marta actively participates by contributing her own ideas and suggestions, thus working with her Maestro to bring to consummation (their) works of art: "I have read *Diana and Tuda* twice. End of the first act—some minor modifications and also at the end of the second act, some acceleration. The third act seems balanced, the final tragedy, well conceived . . . in my opinion the last line should be developed more. (I will read it again.)" (Milan, August 8, 1926; C, p. 30).

Working in close collaboration with him, Marta Abba came to possess an implicit understanding with Pirandello concerning the artistic ideals of the theater. Evidently there was a continuing discussion in their circle about these ideals: After learning of a lecture given by the director Max Reinhardt, Marta wrote a letter to Pirandello summarizing the proceedings and saying she felt it was like something he himself might have said: "What Reinhardt says is very 'Pirandellian,' and what he tells us actors is exceedingly 'true.' So the actor is noble, no longer the hammy actor, as we are used to hearing him called" (Milan, October 3, 1931; C, p. 216).

It is clear that Pirandello depended deeply on Marta's insights into the plays. And we should remember that their collaboration was never merely literary, but also dramatic and theatrical. We must make an effort to conjure up their actual time together—acting, talking, engaging in dialogue, going over parts, rehearsing, discussing character and motivation and expression. A beautiful memory of their private working life together has been recorded by Andrea Pirandello in an article about his childhood with his grandfather:

Many times, we were taken by surprise by strangely enchanted moments. For instance, while we were playing in the garden of the villa Conti in Castiglioncello, we saw, all of a sudden, grandpa and Marta in the green light of the pine grove behind them, in a state of bewitchment that carried them off to another world, distinct from ours. They were performing, or rather, grandpa, sitting or leaning against a pine tree, was giving Marta her cue, and Marta was moving in a surreal space and speaking with a loud voice and gesturing, as if in that cube of air there pulsated another life, between two people, who, although real, were of a different nature than ours. . . . One afternoon, late in spring, grandpa, Marta, my parents, and we three grandchildren, all squeezed into the car driven by Francesco and went for a ride to Monte Cavo, I believe. It was a high hill with a flat top. The grown-ups settled down at a table outside the café up there. Ninní, Giorgio and I went into the woods that covered the sides of the hill. Excited by the new adventure, we went down and down, wandering around until we got lost. In the thick of the woods it was dark, and it must have been getting late. How would we find our way back to the café? All we knew was that we had to climb up again. Somewhat anxious, we set about climbing up, but it was not easy to find the right paths, and it was getting darker and darker. We no longer knew which direction to take, and we had to give each other moral support. From a very great distance, there came to us a long sound like a note held high, which we heard over and over again. It was coming from on high. After a little while, we realized that it was a human voice, a female voice. "Marta!" we cried. It was the extraordinary voice of Marta, powerful, clear, the voice of an actress, which, from the summit, descended upon us like a thread to extricate us from the labyrinth. Guided in this way, we were able to find our way, and we managed to get out. Judging by the anxious faces that greeted us, we could tell that we had spoiled that afternoon of leisure for grandpa and the others. We were not scolded, but they said: "but if it had not been for Marta?" (*Pirandello: L'uomo lo scrittore il teatrante*, p. 147).

This evocative account is bursting with magic. The two are not of this world; their bond transports them into a realm where the rules that commonly regulate relationships between people no longer apply, so that in the midst of family and nature they create an island on which what is denied other mortals becomes possible for them. And it is possible precisely because they have been deprived of what is granted to others: the sweet exhaustion and banality of eros.

'In a state of bewitchment' they 'perform,' that is, they make of the scripted words an instrument not of communication, but of a sort of de-realization, and they themselves thus become capable of magical acts (for instance, Marta saving the children lost in the woods), just as they have become *incapable* of the most basic of human acts. He is the spirit, she the voice; he is the completely disembodied creator, she is his echo resounding in suspended emptiness. It is not by chance that in *The Mountain Giants* Pirandello has Cotrone say about Ilse, the part written for Marta, that "the countess has an enchanted voice." Such was the romance as it was lived, and which was completely analogous to the written romance found in his letters. All that remains of Marta is her voice, just as Echo, in classical myth, was deprived of her physical being while she pined for Narcissus.

The magic of Marta's voice, experienced by the young Andrea as a saving voice from on high, remained undiminished in force well into her eighties. I had the good fortune to discover this when in the 1980s I was interviewing and working with Marta on her correspondence. At that time she played for me a taping of *Find Oneself* she had recently made for broadcast on Italian-Swiss radio. The actress' voice was still so powerful and moving, so natural and fresh, that even when her aging voice cracked or wavered, it always seemed to fit the intensity of the character's emotions perfectly. Her voice brought to life the protagonist of *Find Oneself* vividly, in her struggle to be taken seriously as a modern woman, a person with depth and complexity who is not merely an object of love. It was incredible to me how her skill as an actress remained undiminished in a role that had been written expressly for her so long ago. Marta remained, even a half century after Pirandello's death, her Maestro's Echo.

Out of all the perfect loving portraits that Pirandello crafted for Marta, and out of the hall of mirrors between theater and life, grew the myth that bestowed on the actress the label of ideal interpreter of Pirandello's plays, plays that became a projection of Pirandello's manifold self into the theater and reflected artistic as well as existential anxieties. We can see this total fusion between writer and actress in *As You Desire Me*, the play that fits Marta Abba perhaps better than any other work Pirandello ever wrote for her. *As You Desire Me* remains, even today, the most unforgettable example of collaboration between a playwright and a performer. In this context the actress' statements of the affinity she felt for Pirandello's plays even before she met him become all the more convincing. In *As You Desire Me*, Marta Abba's many masks bring out the torments and the problems of identity which the *Ignota* (unknown woman) hides deep in her soul and projects onto others. These concerns in the play often correspond to problems raised in the letters, and behind the playwright who writes them we glimpse the man who lives and suffers. So too, the torments of the character run parallel to those Marta experienced in real life, and which she shared with Pirandello in her letters. Talking about the reasons that prompted her to leave Berlin, she writes that in Italy at least they recognized her worth, while in Germany nobody knows who she is and nobody understands her when she speaks. In other words, in Germany she had actually been the *Ignota*.

Meanwhile, Pirandello seems at times to attribute other of her problems to the existential crises he thinks she is suffering from: "What did you have, my Marta? Fever? What other disease, besides the serious one of your wounded and discouraged soul?" (Berlin, April 1, 1929; P, p. 57). Delving into Marta's soul, the writer always seems to find reasons why she is worn out, discouraged, or exasperated, just like the characters he creates for her. In turn he would transform his perception of her psychology and its torments into the female roles he wrote for her. In this process, is the author ever disabused of his illusions about who she is, what she feels, why she does what she does? In performing in his plays, and in being the model for their characters, is the actress ever free from the controlling indulgence he exhibits in scripting not only her stage parts but almost her life itself?

The great success of *As You Desire Me* was due to Marta Abba's performance in February 1930, and it resulted in a request from Hollywood to make a movie of the play starring Greta Garbo. Marta, aware of her own contribution, and eager to remind Pirandello of it, writes with tongue in cheek: "You have told me about the offer from the United States regarding *As You Desire Me*, and I'm very happy about it because, as you must admit, I have contributed a little (oh just a little!) to the success of this play" (Salerno, April 4, 1930; C, p. 74).

Even from a great distance (in 1936 Marta is in the United States performing on Broadway) she communicates with Pirandello, suggesting ideas for new plays: "I would like You to probe more deeply into our moment of modern life (I mean "women's lives") and You who are familiar with the American woman's life, could seize the difference, which perhaps is not so different. All women are the same, in their moment of human life, the sufferings are the same, with or without divorce, all have the same aspirations, their feelings are the same. I don't know, but I believe that, observing with your sharp eye, You could follow the life of a woman and perhaps be able to say the right word for this tormented life of ours" (Hotel Pierre, New York City, October 23, 1936; C, p. 387). This suggestion, which anticipates the spirit and principles asserted by the women's movement later in the century, might well have been taken up by Pirandello—especially given the high regard he had for Marta—had he not died a few weeks after the letter was written.

Frustrated Loves: Ideal Interpreter of Pirandello's Theater

The ambiguous nature of Pirandello's sentiments for Marta is revealed by the type of feelings he claims to nourish for her as an actress, feelings that alternate between paternal love and the love of a disappointed lover. It was an attraction that could only be realized through the roles that the author had her live on the stage, lives that made her an impossible object of desire and, at the same time, a mirror of himself. Is it that the actress possessed a particular talent for fitting into the characters that Pirandello created for her? Or is it rather that the Maestro perceived the interior world of a woman as inherently capable of expressing the author's restlessness? Pirandello could not have been unaware of the intense vital and spiritual force of a woman who, with a single glance, could reduce a person to nothing. Once again the ambivalence of this relationship implies that perhaps the label given to Marta Abba, the 'ideal interpreter of Pirandello's theater,' deserves to be reexamined in order for us to comprehend the full richness of its significance.

Pirandello's relationship with Marta Abba did indeed go beyond both the typically intense understanding between author and actress, and the attraction between a man and a woman. In the encounter of these two personalities, there developed a more complex relationship that involved a double form of identification. Not only did the actress identify with Pirandello's female roles, but the author also came to identify with a woman whose very presence represented for him the nearly impossible reconciliation of a potential relationship with his own sexual inhibitions. He wants to feel what Marta feels, to participate totally in everything that she experiences: an identification that is a reduplication, subdivision, and transference of the ego. Hence the desperate attempt, which will torture him right up to the end, to grasp and control her thoughts and feelings: It extends even to the desire to *be* her and, at the same time, to make of her the actress who interprets on stage the profoundest depths of *his* being. (We should not forget that Pirandello from the very beginning identified not only with his male characters but also with his female ones, beginning with Marta Ajala in *The Outcast*). But the desire to become the other inevitably runs up against the reality of that person, who unwittingly becomes overwhelmed by the subject. If, on the one hand, the reduction of the distance between the subject and the other facilitates the process of identification, on the other hand it culminates in a virtual de-realization and dissolution of the actress' true ego.

In this light, the reproaches Pirandello directs toward Marta in his letters can be better understood. In response to these outbursts the actress often has to justify herself for not being able to reply to him at the same frenzied pace. When their respective professional commitments keep them apart, Pirandello, his flood of letters almost always sent by express mail, continues his identification with her, forcing her on a daily basis to read whatever he writes to her and, naturally, to think of him while she writes to him. He expects her to answer with equal frequency: "Write to me, write to me. Think of me. Be conscious of me" (Berlin, April 11, 1929; P, p. 67).

Marta is clearly overwhelmed by the sheer volume of his letters, and she makes him aware that she cannot possibly reciprocate: "What I do know is that I always remember things confusedly in answering you …afterwards, when I read your letters, I realize that I did not answer what was asked; and I become so exhausted that I throw myself, drained, onto the bed after writing a few lines […] I don't know how I could possibly answer all your volumes of letters, which are, for the most part, volumes of useless words that make me sad, irritate me, and upset me" (Messina, April 12, 1930; C, pp. 77-8). When he presses her with constant accusations, she responds with exasperation: "I have received so many letters from you, and there is always some reproach for me, that in good conscience I know I don't deserve. I live the life of a dog. I'm so exhausted I can't go on, and then, on top of it all, I get your reproaches" (Turin, January 5, 1931; C, p. 128). To defend herself from his onslaughts Marta pleads physical exhaustion and psychological distraction (which, probably unwittingly, only feeds into the Maestro's techniques of subtle and tortuous manipulation): "I feel that your reproaches and accusations are undeserved, especially since I feel my head is off somewhere sometimes, I don't feel it there on my shoulders, utter exhaustion, which prevents me from put my ideas in order […]" (Turin, January 15, 1931; C, p. 132).

It is clear that in her real life the actress was reluctant to become what he would have liked her to be, since this would have entailed the renunciation of her self and her own identity. In this sense, she feels the insistent pace of his correspondence to be the exact opposite of a real relationship, in which the other becomes truly and authentically other. If the writer intended the letters as an expression of love, they end up being quite the reverse. Without the other love does not exist. Rather, all that remains is desperate and endless reflection. It is not Marta but her visible shadow that becomes his interlocutor, an interlocutor who in turn identifies with the writer's own shadow and becomes a part, a figment, of his own personality.

This identification between author and actress can thus only be realized on stage: the only form of life permitted the actress is the one that she and she alone is willing to give through the theater. For Pirandello, this is the only way that will allow him to continue living through Marta, since she is destined to repeat the characters and actions that the author created for her. Such is the implication of his letter of September 25, 1928: "As far as I am concerned, after fulfilling my mission, I'll get out of your way, and my spirit will go on living in you, my dear Marta, if you choose to keep on giving me life in your memory!" (P, p. 25). In light of these extremely private hopes of the author for a kind of metempsychosis through the actress' performances of his plays, the plot of *Diana and Tuda* takes on a new resonance, revealing still more than it seems when considered on its own.

To what extent was the actress conscious of the extreme role accorded to her by the Maestro even outside of the theater? How should we interpret the female protagonist's suicide, presented on stage by Marta in *Diana and Tuda*, if not as an inextricable convergence of identification and rivalry that renders all possible defenses inoperative—if not as a manifestation of impotence? As always, Pirandello's obstinate silence on the question of sexuality arouses suspicion. When sexual situations arise, they are always considered degrading and horrifying. But despite Pirandello's rigorous discretion, the traces of desire in the correspondence assume their own explicit dimension, which decisively confirms the writer's conflicts. These conflicts are of great significance precisely because they are never made explicit in his works, including the correspondence.

The Romance Novel of Life

It is no accident, therefore, that the protagonists in almost all of Pirandello's later plays are women. In each of his attempts to create the other, who lives splendidly in the impassioned woman "with reddish hair," Pirandello always reverts to the tormented meanderings of the identification process, returning to the source of his original inhibitions, to the anguish of sexuality as abandonment (an ego, weak and divided, fears love as a mortal risk, as the loss of the self). The situation reaches a dimension that is beyond a normal desire for the other sex; in fact, the identification with the female character goes beyond the condition, more or less conscious, of his own sexuality, and reflects a desire to worship the objects she loves, to feel what she feels. To worship the same objects and to repeat the same movements are only possible in love's game of identification: "I am returning from the *Aida* [an Italian restaurant in Berlin]; there were very few people there maybe because it is a very beautiful spring day.... Naturally my meal was sadder than ever, there all by myself, at the usual spot, in our little niche. I sit where you always sat, on the sofa; I lean back just like you used to do; but as for eating, I eat next to nothing." (Berlin, March 17, 1929; L, p. 70). He writes in a similar vein the following year:

> I am, as you can see, at the Vendome, and I occupy room 5, the same one you had, and I sleep in the same bed in which you slept during your Parisian vacation. This way I feel a little less far away from you. Here in these rooms I have your picture of that time, with the two big straw hats, the white one and the black one—which suited you so well —and the white and pale blue dress with the mantelet.... I see you here lying down on the couch of green *peluche* near the little desk I am now writing at, facing the drawing-room window ... I see you while you talk to that hateful Torre, who is eating you up with those enamel eyes of a swindling fake magician, and I cringe when I notice that you are smiling at him in a different way from the way you smile at good old Camillo Antona-Traversi. ... My trouble is that I notice everything and I suffer because

of everything ... though I really should give no importance to things that have none for you ... but when devotion is so complete and absolute and when a person doesn't live except through the life that is given him by another person, if even a minimal part of this life fails him for one moment, this is what unfortunately happens! This is why, Marta, you should forgive me and not feel offended. It is pain and not reproach; it is a confession of a weakness and nothing else. I deserve your compassion, which you can grant me only if you understand the reason for my suffering (Paris, March 12, 1930; P, pp. 108-9).

The inclination to substitute himself for the loved one, to fill her place, reveals both the vulnerability and the intense desperation that he feels at her loss. It is the impossibility of completely realizing such a desire that in itself proves to be consoling, since it provides an emotional limit that relieves the imagination of further responsibilities. In real life, desire can unleash aggressive forms of jealousy for what the other feels—feelings which are denied to the subject. By building a prison around the actress, Pirandello attempts to create situations in which she would be blocked from sexual fulfillment, both in real life and on the stage, since such realization would evade his control and make him unable to inhabit her feelings. His only recourse is the theater, where he can make her experience what he experiences and can thus attain, through the fiction of the performance, the only possible (albeit precarious) form of possession.

Certainly Pirandello was well aware that sexually he would never be able to appropriate her sensations. On the other hand, how many times in Pirandello's work (e.g. *One Knows Not How, Either One or No One*) do we encounter moments of latent homosexuality, all played out through the love-hate relationship that operates as a defense against sexual matters, since the author considers them to be a form of degradation? In fact, Pirandello harbored a deep-seated horror of such matters, akin to the fear of the "beast," which from time to time tries to break loose, and which he always tries to keep under control: "I am petrified to be left alone with myself," he writes to Marta on July 5, 1928. "All the beasts of my cage wake up to tear me to pieces. And I do not know how to placate them. What an anguish to watch life with this feeling I have, that I am deprived of it. I press against my chest, as tight as I can, a consoling Image" (Nettuno [Rome], July 5, 1928; P, p. 18). The "Image" is, of course, a photograph of Marta.

Just as in the theater, where Pirandello configures images and facts of social life around a character in order to reveal the mechanisms of conscience, the capacity to react, the response to the system, and the possibility of individual redemption, so in the letters he has the need to situate around Marta—actress and woman, concrete and abstract heroine,—all the images of his own life. But, beyond the constraining structures of Pirandello's art, the letters written from Berlin—and above all those written just after she left on March 13, 1929—possess all the ingredients of a love story, and reveal the great depth of Pirandello's passion for Marta Abba, as well as revealing the torment and frustration of a man with the added disadvantage of being elderly. In these pages Pirandello brings together and evaluates the many facets of his own life. His assessment is deprecatory, and not even his worldwide successes or his recognition of them can place his life in a more positive light: "Well, I am an Academician of Italy. But I remain, my dear Marta, the very same poor man as before, whom no prize, no honor will ever be able to compensate for the loss of your company, which alone would have made me enjoy the honor, and more for your sake than for mine" (Berlin, March 22, 1929; P, p. 39).

Sometimes it is as if his desire puts him under Marta's power, and her shadow impels him towards elusive goals, pushing him from what he is toward what he will become. Alone, he lacks the rhetorical devices to communicate directly what might allow him to escape the shame afflicting him. Lacking the ability to express his desire, his sexuality breaks out into its opposite, a heartfelt frustration of desire, which, when it is not indulged, becomes pathological. His fear of sex seems to have always won out; his disgust for the flesh and its blind needs finds clear expression in this beach "scene" described to Marta: "Then I went down to the beach briefly. What a meat market! Some women…the beach is narrow, and the sea is eating it away more year after year. All clustering together—men and women—in that little dirty sandpit, filthy. Some of these scenes! Some of these expositions! I went back up to my balcony, nauseous (Nettuno, July 9, 1928; L, p. 42). These "expositions" seen on the beach are nothing but the object of his desire in its 'nude' manifestation, and for this reason they become unbearable, since they remind him of the responsibility he bears for confronting the other, especially that ultimate other—the human body. Inevitably the letters, precisely at the points where they become witness to a love story, gain vitality from his fear of sex, and thus fit in quite well with a constantly striking feature in Pirandello's works. The writer loves with a desperate love. Marta was as rich in talent as she was endowed with distinctive feminine qualities that set her apart from the common lot. But he is afraid and "horrified" (a word he uses constantly) by the possibility that this absolute and possessive feeling has to be expressed through the body.

When Marta abandons him in Berlin, after their failure to establish profitable theater and film ventures in the booming German film industry (this critical event in their relationship will recur several times in the following chapters), Pirandello starts writing long letters on an almost daily basis. Having collapsed into sullen desperation after Marta's departure, he nostalgically recalls those months spent with the actress, thus breathing life into the most tormented chapter of the entire correspondence. He knows that in Italy it will be impossible to have Marta constantly by his side, as she had been during their stay in Germany. The letters of this period are clear proof of this. At first glance, they may seem like a lover's lament, one of many throughout the history of literature, but the famous playwright cannot believe himself. The situation in the correspondence reflects the typical structure of Pirandello's plays. It is indeed a narration that, although moving in a very logical and rectilinear direction, runs up against its own opposite: unpredictable events giving rise to existential crises. As the play unfolds, the thread becomes entangled between the logic on which the plot is based and the forces acting against it. The entire correspondence, in fact, moves between two surfaces. On one level are the concrete aspects of everyday life, which are represented by domestic problems (for instance, his daughter and son-in-law cheating him, his worries concerning the future of his sons Fausto and Stefano, etc.) and by the many difficulties that originate in the trying world of show business, which then become the occasion for his humor and laughter. The other level consists of abstractions (love, existence, jealousy—all feelings that, at least for the last ten years of his life, revolve around Marta) and becomes the occasion for weeping.

As soon as Marta's train leaves the station in Berlin, Pirandello returns home and writes the first letter in which he fully describes his anguish: "I returned home, threw myself into the armchair near the window, and remained there, I don't know how long, in the dark, with only the glimmer coming from the street lamps down in the square. The silence from the adjacent room, where until a few hours ago you had lived, was filling me with a sense of death. I wept out my sorrow for hours and hours. Forgive me if I tell you this. I was alone and able to cry" (Berlin, March 14, 1929; P, p. 30). Writing again a few days later, he confesses that from now on he will cry in silence, and he will not mention his tears. But in spite of his promise, tears do flow again, flooding the course of his correspondence as well as his plays: "He was so sad, so disconsolate that, just from listening to him talk—and I was so alone, myself—I was so wretched, without anything worthwhile in sight—I began weeping, weeping—not dreaming that my tears, tears for myself, for my own desolation..." says the *Ignota*, the unknown woman, in the second act of *As You Desire Me*. The character clearly describes in the third person the disconsolate aspects of the author's own psyche.

Elsewhere, Pirandello confesses that in a moment of desperation, without knowing what to do, he would drink a glass of water to quench his thirst. Water becomes the medium through which desperation is transposed into writing, through which the wall of silence created by the pain is shattered into words, which, as we well know, serve as a substitute for love. One drizzly evening Pirandello is slowly walking home alone. He is so absorbed in his thoughts of Marta that he gets completely soaked. Later, alone in his room, he listens to the ticking of the little alarm clock Marta had once given him. He closes his eyes, imagining it on her nightstand, and remembers the time when, after winding the clock, he used to say good night to her and return to his room. Once again he bursts into tears. It is a delirium of tears, a drenching of himself and the objects that remind him of her—a kind of orgasm of tears.

On the day before Easter, frustrated because he has not received a letter from Marta in more than a week, Pirandello decides to send her a telegram. As he says, it was "such a sad Easter day, rainy and foggy like winter!" (Berlin, April 1, 1929; P, p. 56). By coincidence, on Easter day Marta writes him a letter in which she says it had also rained in Milan, causing her "a little indisposition." The very laws of nature seem at times to accompany the lovers' own whirlwinds. Pirandello replies to her: "Today is Sunday and it has been raining all morning. The sky is gloomy and keeps my soul in a somber mood" (Berlin, April 7, 1929; L, p. 118).

Pirandello's response to a letter Marta had written during a fit of desperate frustration belongs to that breathless group of letters after she had left Berlin. This group constitutes in itself a shorter love story within the entire body of his correspondence:

> Marta, my Marta, your cry for help on Saturday evening has arrived at this very moment! I knew that when you left and went back to Italy like that you would end up in such a state. All the stronger was my chagrin when I saw you leave and get away from me, because I felt I could not and should not do anything to prevent it—although I knew. At that time every word of mine, every attempt at persuasion, would have looked selfish on my part; that is, that I did not want to let you go for my own sake, so as not to be left in this horrible solitude; and also because it was clear that you had lost your confidence in me and that you thought you would be safer trusting your father's ridiculous conceit and your sister Cele's infinitely silly

conceit. Oh, my Marta, my humiliation for all this! My dejection at not being able to confront you with a convincing reason against your decision to leave—a factual proof, a signed contract, something that could be touched by your hands and give weight and strength to my words!

But it's useless to tell you all this now. Right now you need to be relieved of the despair filling your soul, and to be consoled, my Marta, by the person who loves you and does not live for anyone but you . . . . Who can have taken your place? Your place on the Italian stage, for a while, can stay empty, but it cannot be taken over by any other actress, *ever*: because none of them even stands as high as your knee, and you are you, unmistakable, insuppressible, irreplaceable. You—with your way of being, feeling, thinking, expressing yourself, speaking, moving: which is only yours and cannot belong to anybody else; which makes you MARTA ABBA, a name signed by destiny and entrusted to glory. But this *Marta* should not be *marta*, this MARTA, without these fits of discouragement, should keep herself worthy of her destiny! And I am here to tell you this; I am here to confirm that her destiny (remember!) *has been foretold*; and Marta should not turn away from that *predestination*! I am her man; the man her destiny assigned to her; I am her Destiny, and I am nothing else; and this is so true, that without this, that is, without you, I am nothing anymore. Do you understand this, my Marta? (Berlin, March 28, 1929; P, pp. 47-8).

This is on a Thursday—he grovels at her feet by elevating her to the stars and linking his destiny to hers. But by Saturday Pirandello decides to reverse the terms, insisting that she has cruelly abandoned her only possible source of comfort and satisfaction. He reproaches her and ramps up his accusations against Cele:

Comfort from me, after you left me the way you did? When

> those who are around you, your family, to whom you preferred to go, neither knew how nor could give it to you? While I alone was capable of giving it to you here—and now more than ever, after what happened, after what is still to come—I alone could give comfort, had you stayed here, as you should have. Your nature is too impressionable, Marta, and your sister Cele more than anybody else is the one who knows how to take advantage of it. You give in, without even knowing it, to her suggestions, which are all harmful for you; she has led you always where she wanted; you have always ended up doing what she wanted (Berlin, March 30, 1929; P, p. 52).

The very next day he retreats, returning to tones of apology, supplication, and love:

> I confess, it seemed to me unfair that, while complaining that *you do not have a word of comfort from anybody*, you still wanted and expected such word *particularly from me*—although I was so disheartened and desolate because of you! How could comfort come from me when all my life had gone away with you? When here with me nothing but regret was left, continuously, every single hour, every single minute? The only comfort that could come from me was knowing that there is one person in the world who loves you more than himself, one who does not live, who cannot live without you, who therefore lives for you (Berlin, Easter Day, 1929; P, p. 55).

Pirandello filled page after page describing his passions for Marta and tracing the entire repertoire of traditional love. But these alternate with pages evincing disillusionment, whether in reaction to her overly reserved answers or to her delayed answers to his neurotically punctual letters. He continues this existence day in and day out, suffering a constant inner struggle while waiting for Marta's answers, which always come too late. He also includes detailed descriptions of his bodily ills (often symptoms

The Romance Novel of Life

that are psychosomatic in nature), with the idea of making Marta feel sorry for him and guilty. Pirandello generally begins by saying that he has not received news from her and that he hopes to receive some letters that might pacify him the following day. Then he begins to enumerate signs of irritation: "I don't feel good here, I can't sleep at night; the bed is hard, the chairs are hard; and it rains and rains and rains" (Rome, September 23, 1928; L, p. 51). Later, in a description of his various maladies, he gives a detailed analysis and confesses that:

> What has been worrying me most for a number of nights is that I cannot sleep anymore. I had so far always found in sleep a respite from all the pains of my life—which have been many—and a certain tonic for my physical health. I'd certainly have gone mad if all the torments of my heart and all the turmoil of my mind had not found rest during the night. Now, for several nights, my eyes remain open in the darkness, and the hours become enormous; I shiver and shake and—frightening thing—if my eyes get veiled by an almost-white drowsiness, my body feels as if it were whining, speaking. Like in the past ...
>
> I am not angry with anybody; I rebel against insomnia itself; I make an effort to sleep, forbidding myself to think, to feel (Berlin, April 8, 1929; P, p. 64).

Pirandello clearly insinuates that all this is Marta's responsibility. But he goes on to explain that he cannot do otherwise: "the body does not want to; the beast does not get tired and, although whipped, it still does not want to; its blood is all churned up; its heart beats too quickly and does not want to; maybe it conceals a disease that I don't know about yet; but if it cannot help itself, I certainly can't" (p. 64). A continuous crescendo of torment leads him inevitably toward tragic conclusions that will not allow him to recover, as he lives out the entire pathological novelistic fantasy of pain and suffering. He will die because she left him: "Because now, after three years of living close by you, I feel that without you, although I try very hard to resist, I am dying. I am dying because I no longer know what to do with my life; in this horrible loneliness there is no more sense for me in living—neither value nor purpose" (Berlin, March 20, 1929; P, p. 37).

Here the unbreakable link between his illness and the impossibility of love becomes clear, as if the former were a consequence of the latter, while instead it is his deep-seated illness that has caused his deadly inability to love: "Yesterday I was in bed for the whole day with a high fever and an upset stomach. I probably caught a cold in my stomach. But it's nothing serious. No doubt I'll be completely over it by tomorrow, and I'll go back to Rome. I can't wait for these days of exile to be over. I don't get any rest and I can hardly even breathe anymore. If only I could work! I cannot. I have been without food for two days; and this heat, my weakness, and the flies..." (Nettuno [Rome], July 8,1928; P, p. 18).

In response to his endless bouts of epistolary doom and desperation, Marta at times comes to his rescue by attempting to ease his soul back into the romance of living:

> Open up, extend, Maestro, room, more room, I should not want your thoughts to revolve too constantly about this axis of life and death, this Life which must not take on substance, lest it become Death. This seems to me what I have understood. No, Maestro, I should like it that you extend yourself further, both in poetic feeling and in love [...] Do not be afraid to be no longer Pirandello, or another Pirandello, you who are at one and the same time one and one hundred thousand, be so in fact, to embrace everything, including the beauty that fills our spirits with wonder and dismay (Salsomaggiore, May 28, 1930; C, pp. 104-5).

A Rigid Program

Lingering even behind professional exchanges there lie concealed in Pirandello's letters the latent tension and anxiety stemming from his amorous feelings for Marta, the woman who not only gave life to his characters on the stage, but who also became a mirror for his own desperate emotions. The theater, from which he demands everything, also takes everything from him, and the further away the woman, the more malleable she becomes for facilitating his transformation of life on the stage. Anyone reading his letters will quickly become familiar with the games Pirandello uses in his attempts to manipulate Marta's feelings and reactions. His bewilderment intensifies when he suspects that she could live and be happy without him, when he fears that she could find pleasure in another, and that he would lose the role he has assumed in her eyes. Often ostensibly preoccupied with Marta's future career, he is actually attempting to exercise a repressive control over her. He wants to subject the actress so that she cannot escape even for an instant from the total sacrifice to art which he has planned for her. This may be one reason why the myth of *The Mountain Giants* will accompany the vicissitudes of their relationship for many years. In that play, on the subject of her sacrifices to the dead author's work, Ilse at one point says:

> It was a sacred duty for me! A young friend of his (*designating her husband*), a poet, came to read a work that he was writing—he said for me—but he really had no hope, because I had left the stage. The work struck me as being so beautiful that—yes, that's right, I got excited over it immediately. But I understand what he was driving at. (It doesn't take long for a woman to notice these things—when someone has an idea about her, I mean.) He wanted to lure me back to my former life with his tempting play. But it was not for the sake of the work; it was for himself, to make me his...I felt that if I disappointed him right away, he would never have finished the work. And because it was so beautiful, not only did I not disappoint him, but I actually nourished his illusion till the very end. When the work was finished, I withdrew from that fire, though I was already burning of it. How can you not understand it, seeing me in this painful condition? He is right: I

could never free myself from it. The life which I denied him, I had to devote to his work. And he himself understood it (*designating her husband*) and consented that I return to the stage in order to fulfill this sacred duty of mine. For this play alone!

CROMO: Consecration and martyrdom!...But don't you understand that he is not dead for her? She wants him to live! Here she is in shreds like a beggar; she is dying and she is causing all of us to die of it just so he, the author, may still live!

His desire for this kind of control is particularly well illustrated in his description of a "rigid program" that he envisions for Marta:

And also about studying, the two of us together, you and me alone; opening up my mind and pouring all my knowledge into you in a few days, to enrich your spirit with all the necessary literary trends; studying French in addition to German, to give you a command of at least two languages beyond Italian, for your tours abroad. All the above *must* happen again, if we are to know how to do things the way they should be done: with perseverance, willpower, without getting lost and without deviations. You should by all means set up for yourself a rigid program, to be followed point by point, with absolute discipline and utmost precision. You spend too much time in front of the mirror, thinking how best to make yourself up. You do not have all that much time to lose: you should no longer do it. Anyway, it is useless; because you do not need it, you are always beautiful without it. You must get up early, always at the same time; and never go to bed later than 12:30 a.m. One hour is sufficient for the morning bath and getting dressed; breakfast follows, then the study of your roles, as you used to do; in the afternoon, languages; but your studies must include also the plays, to grasp their deepest spirit and squeeze out of them all the life they want to have, and the meaning and the value they have; and also all the effects that can be extracted from them in performance—never arbitrary, always legitimate, although personal, because they result from being illuminated by your very special intelligence. There shouldn't ever be time for boredom and for regrets; we should constantly fill up our day with work. Life will not appear empty anymore; we will not have the feeling of having lost it, if every day we find it again within us, awake and ready to nourish our passion for art, which is never satiated, never tires, and is never completely fulfilled (Berlin, March 29, 1929; P, p. 50).

Pirandello wrote this letter not long after Marta had left him alone in Berlin, and in it he seeks above all to restore a close relationship that is now lost. The significance of this "rigid program" he outlines for Marta becomes clearer in light of the timeline of events leading up to it. The three-year run of the Teatro d'Arte, which took Pirandello as its director around the world, accompanied by Marta Abba, ended after a disappointing Italian tour in the summer of 1928. Except for during the company's summer breaks, their correspondence falls almost entirely silent between 1925 and the first half of 1928. The company's financial situation had been precarious for some time as a consequence of bad administration. But on their return from South America, with the company collapsing under the weight of its debts, they tried in November of 1927 to make a comeback in Italy. After its last performances in Viareggio in August 1928, the company of Teatro d'Arte of Rome foundered. Disillusioned and exhausted, but always ready to begin again, Pirandello decided to move to Germany and take Marta with him. At this point the correspondence starts up again for a short time (he is in Rome, she in Milan) while the two are preparing for the move to Germany.

Then, in the middle of March 1929, after Marta returns to Italy from Berlin, the correspondence resumes on a regular basis, except of course when the two are together—during Pirandello's rare visits to Italy, for example, or when they are both in Paris. The letters Pirandello writes from Germany, which we already explored partially above, constitute the most copious part of the entire correspondence. They show the immense burden of solitude borne by this "traveler without bags" (as he often describes himself), who lives first in Berlin and then in Paris, in hotels and small apartments, always in a transitory state. Disappointed by the discouraging outcome of the last few plays (*Diana and Tuda, Each One to His Own*), Pirandello wants to establish, from abroad, a new and more positive image of himself. He regards the movie business as a golden opportunity. This is the period, as we noted earlier, in which Pirandello works on the screenplay of the *Six Characters*.

After the failure of *Tonight We Improvise* (May 1930), Pirandello leaves Berlin for good and moves to Paris for a few years. Even from there he continues to watch over Marta, for whom he writes *Trovarsi* (partly in Paris and partly in the Tuscan resort town of Castiglioncello during the summer of 1932), which the actress performs in November of that same year in Naples. But in spite of his efforts, Pirandello, as is clear from reading between the lines of the letters, still feels that he is searching for some great new success, especially after his disappointing experiences in Germany and in Hollywood in 1932 with the movie version of *As You Desire Me*. Nor could Marta's not insignificant successes, achieved (thanks to the precious counseling of the Maestro) with the company she herself managed and with which she toured Italy from 1929 to 1934, lift him out of his state of discouragement. Even in the depths of his pessimism, however, he remained convinced of his ability to create the ultimate play, a goal that he seems to have been pursuing in the long and tormented gestation of *The Mountain Giants*. He regarded this play as a means of ensuring the triumph that he had always planned for his actress, not so much for himself as for her, and certainly not out of an impulse of generosity, but as part and parcel of the plan to 'possess' her definitively (and not without the intrusion of financial considerations, which would ratify the triumph and enable them to live in the fullness of creativity).

Indeed, the letters he writes describing the intense imagination that went into composing *The Mountain Giants* attest to a creative spirit reaching the peak of its powers and insight, and seem to border on, if not

The Romance Novel of Life

to enter outright, the ineffable realms of mystical experience. Here, as always, Marta is ever-present, a Beatrice to his soul's wandering pilgrim:

> I do believe that I am composing my masterpiece, *The Mountain Giants* with a fervor and a trepidation that I can't express. I feel I have climbed to heights where my voice finds unheard-of sounds. My art has never before been so full, so varied and unpredictable: so truly like a feast for the spirit and for the eyes—all like shining pulsations and as fresh as dew. . . . I'm writing for you. I wouldn't be able to write one more word should your divine, inspiring image abandon me for one instant. I follow this image of you, in the situations in which I placed it, and little by little it finds for me the words and creates for me the scenes, and carries me ahead—suggesting, showing me what the other characters must say, what they must do in order to answer to its vagaries, to placate or increase its anxieties, to make out of the contrasting characters the supreme harmony of composition. Without being aware of it, from so far away, perhaps not even thinking a little bit about me, taken by other thoughts, by other preoccupations, you are doing my work. . . . I have all my life in you; you are my art; without your breath it dies. You are creating, and you do not know it, with all the power of your art, with the tones of your inimitable voice, with the splendor of your eyes that find the look for every passion; you are creating with the ardor that has come to me from your mind, from your heart, from all your person, so that I might transfer it into the work that I am writing through you and that is not mine but yours: *your creation* (Paris, February 10, 1931; P, pp. 172-3, original emphasis).

And a few days later:

> You'll see what *The Mountain Giants* is like! It has everything, it's an orgy of fantasy! The lightness of a cloud passing over the depth of an abyss; powerful laughter exploding among the

tears, like thunder in the midst of storms; and everything suspended, whatever I have done so far; I am touching the peak, you'll see! But it's you, only you who are touching it, my Marta! With all your soul, which rejoices in me and creates inside me that sense of a fable in which all the characters breathe, and the words bloom like flowers that seem astonished at being born. There is somebody, my Marta, who is living your life, and you don't know it. Your true life!" (Paris, February 16, 1931; P, p. 175).

The final Marta, the truest Marta of Pirandello's imagining, is thus the Ilse (the incarnation of the ultimate sacrifice of the self to art) of *The Mountain Giants*, a work that by its very nature could not be finished, and not simply because of the author's death. Pirandello's was a path with no exit. In time, as submission began to replace hope, he wrote to the actress: "I must fervently hope, my dear Marta, that I have little time left to live: I truly do not wish to prolong it. I feel every desire vanishing from me, and everything, my very body, is a burden to me" (Rome, December 9, 1935; P, p. 304).

But his inexhaustible vitality does sometimes overpower his discouragement, and creates the hope that he might still succeed in the film industry, which he perceives as a new and powerful factory turning out money and success. Meanwhile, in 1934, Pirandello chairs the meetings of the Convention organized in Rome in honor of Alessandro Volta. For this occasion, he directs *Jorio's Daughter (La figlia di Jorio)*, a tribute to d'Annunzio, with whom he had had some disputes in the past but whom he is now willing to embrace, since he feels that they were both equally marginalized by the Fascist regime that was then at its peak. And, as if recreating the early days of the Teatro d'Arte, on this occasion Pirandello experiences a new triumph as a director, when Marta Abba gives a wonderful performance in the role of Mila di Codra. At various points in the letters, he outlines his projects, which are always numerous, and hopes in his heart of hearts that he can recreate with Marta, albeit in a different form, the ideal situation they experienced during the years of the Teatro d'Arte, which coincided with the high point of their personal relationship.

Much more often, however, we get the sense that the stranglehold of time inexorably and silently suffocates him as he resists like a prisoner in a futile rebellion. He knows that with Marta he has reached the pinnacle of his desires, and that the dream of the last daring flight that he wanted to experience with her has disintegrated into regret at his not being able to live in another world, in another time. Love, glimpsed late in life and viewed fondly as a panacea in his last few years, rather than relieving him from the "pain of existence," has instead accentuated the inevitability of that pain—not because the love was unreciprocated, but because Pirandello had never truly sought reciprocity, constrained as he was by the impotence of self-reflexivity and the fragmentation of his ego. Just as with Mrs. Leuca in *The Pain of Living Thus*, the long novella which he revised heavily during his relationship with Marta, life without love pours itself out until it becomes transparent. But life in the face of love runs the risk of the trauma of sexuality and of interaction with the other. Faced with the impossibility of realizing his desire, the author, just like his characters, is obliged to accept his own impotence. They both collapse, spent, and live only long enough to realize that they are dying.

But 1934 is also the year in which Pirandello receives the Nobel Prize. Even for this occasion the letters to Marta show all the turmoil of a man who is unable to savor fully such a grand recognition: something is still lacking, namely, the actress' presence. In the letters he wrote at this time, which we might expect to be full of pride, we see instead disappointment that Marta, who was supposed to accompany him to the Nobel ceremony in Stockholm, withdrew at the last moment, offering only a feeble excuse: "As for our trip, dear Maestro, I'm afraid it's out of the question. After Amelia had bent over backwards to organize it, the other day, despite my desire to go ahead with the plans, she told me that it would not perhaps be such a good idea for her to undertake another trip since only a few weeks had elapsed since the first one. You know that she wasn't feeling well on her trip to Vienna and Budapest. In short, Amelia Valdameri's withdrawal makes it impossible for me to go" (Milan, December 4, 1934; C, p. 268). In reality, Marta Abba herself admitted to me in conversation in 1984 that her decision not to accompany Pirandello to Stockholm was prompted by her family's concern for propriety and appearances.

Right up to the very end, the correspondence makes frequent mention of the possibility of contracts for new films. In spite of Pirandello's personal view of (and reservations about) the film industry, he continued to harbor up through the last days of his life the hope that it could become the only true new source of success and financial gain for Marta and him. Just before his death, he was still entertaining the hope of making a Hollywood movie based on *Six Characters*. As the director of the movie he wanted Max Reinhardt, who by that time had moved to the United States because of racial persecutions in Germany. Earlier, in fact, Pirandello had criticized Reinhardt as a stage director on many occasions, and it is no secret that the unfavorable portrayal of the stage director in *Tonight We Improvise* (1930) was inspired by Reinhardt.

We can clearly see Pirandello's enthusiasm for his movie projects in the correspondence: "Today I went for lunch at the Adlon, invited by Otto Kahn, who is now in Berlin. As you know, Otto Kahn is one of the wealthiest persons in the world. . . . He wanted to learn about all my ideas for the cinema, and when I explained them to him, he was *enthusiastic*: enthusiastic about *Six Characters*" (Berlin, April 29, 1929; P, pp. 76-7; original emphasis). Three years later, in 1932, while *As You Desire Me* was in production, *Six Characters* was still waiting in the wings: "News: the most serious is the decision Thalberg [director at Metro-Goldwyn Mayer] seems to have reached, of doing the film of *Six Characters* after finishing *As You Desire Me*, about which Lawrence (the representative of Metro-Goldwyn) reports wonders; he says that Garbo's interpretation is *amazing*, and that the film will be *sensational*" (Paris, May 4, 1932; P, p. 227). We will explore Pirandello's experiences with the cinema more fully in the following chapter.

Jealousy, uncertainty, fear both present and future, life and theater, are so many states of mind that illustrate the romantic atmosphere in which Pirandello lives out his feelings for Marta Abba, and that confirm the critical role the actress played in the last ten years of his life. Their correspondence illuminates some of the writer's weaknesses as well as his strong moral sense, which caused him so much suffering. The letters both reveal and conceal, with the result that certain aspects of his 'friendship' with Marta still remain shrouded in mystery. The playwright's passion for Marta is tinged with fears that make him a prisoner of the same precarious situation. In the end it seems as though he derived a sort of masochistic pleasure from this self-destructive torment, and it kept him suspended in a game that could have no resolution.

Chapter 2

PIRANDELLIAN THEATER UNDER FASCISM

That Pirandello was in many respects out of sync with the Italy of his times is well known. His long, self-imposed sojourns abroad tell us much about his sense of the oppression of the constraints of Italian life in those years. We can see in his correspondence with Marta that she too was out of step with the times, not only because of her choice of theatrical parts and repertoire, but also because of her free interpretations of characters that provoked the fury of critics who were not always disposed to accept new forms of interpretation, especially from an actress whom many considered young and inexperienced.

The actress also had a social conscience with respect to the theater industry and its conditions of labor and organization. It was evident that the Fascist Corporations, with their theatrical associations depending on and tied to men involved in national politics, were not particularly concerned with the needs of theater, with society's need for theater, and, most importantly, with theater as a space for artistic expression. Marta and Pirandello, on the other hand, both shared a strong interest in preserving the freedom and vitality of the theater and in the creation of innovative works of artistic imagination.

They and others in theater were particularly concerned about the so-called "Trust" system. This policy systematically excluded independent and autonomous theatrical companies, which staged repertoires not imposed by the strictly commercial, and government-ideological, interests that governed the monopoly over theaters, repertories, and companies administered by the Trust, which ultimately meant the Suvini and Zerboni corporation. On many occasions Marta tried to make Mussolini aware of the difficulties the newly emerging system was creating for artists.

Pirandello also had a very conflicted relationship with Fascism and with Mussolini himself. Early Fascism (1922-1925), originally a complex and heterogeneous political movement, was still far from being transformed into a dictatorship. Revolutionary impulses and confused aspirations for social change, reactions of the status quo and needs for order, desires for freedom and more conservative tendencies, antidemocratic and anticlerical proclamations, and obeisance to existing institutions—all these came together to form an explosive mixture in which discontented veterans from World War I, young idealists, opportunists, futurists, revolutionary union activists and promoters of armed bands of union-busters, republicans, and faithful subjects of the king were all held together by one man, Mussolini, who seemed to embody all of these contradictions. For an equal variety of reasons, Pirandello watched with growing interest, which soon developed into open assent, the movement Mussolini had begun.

Many times before and after he became a member of the Fascist Party (in September 1924, a few months after the Socialist leader Giacomo Matteotti's assassination on June 10), Pirandello said that he had no interest in politics, and that he only became a member of the Fascist Party to aid in the renovation and reconstruction of Italy. In this way he managed to make enemies on both sides. Although his party membership looked suspicious to opponents of Fascism, he was nevertheless a lukewarm partisan, which led to Party leaders being displeased with him as well. Thus his position of 'apolitical' party-membership might well have looked to both sides as a self-serving position of convenience. But clearly Pirandello was not completely comfortable: in him coexisted the crisis of the twentieth century, the end of the old certainties, the anguish and absurdity of life, and the fragility of forms (whether political or psychological). Although Pirandello has often been presented as an exponent of Fascist revolutionary heroism, he belongs among those extraordinary minds (including Celine, Pound, and others) whose complexity of thought goes far beyond the narrow confines of political party geography and popular ideology. It can only be said with oversimplification that they 'belong' to this or that political movement.

The Argentina Incident

By 1926, already in the first letters he wrote to Marta, Pirandello expresses his intention to go abroad. This he finally did in October 1928, moving to Germany, the country he knew from his university studies in Bonn forty years earlier. Why, over the course of these two years, was Pirandello considering leaving Italy, if his acceptance of Fascism were so clear cut? 1927 in particular seems to have been a turning point in his political attitudes. An incident during his tour of South America with the Teatro d'Arte di Roma had serious repercussions in Italy. The incident was provoked by some revelations Pirandello himself made to the press and to anti-Fascist political refugees living in South America. Published and misinterpreted by the local press, Pirandello's words reached Italy and provoked harsh reactions from the chief secretary of the Fascist party, who regarded them as a criticism of the regime. There are many different accounts of this notorious event, but the principal events are clear. Pirandello's original statements to the South American press were an attempt to clarify his link to the government in light of its financial backing of the theatrical company. In this regard he told reporters in Argentina that he was not there as a representative of the Italian government, nor as a member of a specific party. He added that he did not want to be considered a politician on a propaganda campaign, but simply an artist whose only goal was to travel around the world supporting his works.

Some critics have read this statement in a non-Fascist vein, especially since throughout the trip Pirandello gave lectures, and made other statements, that always insisted on his being an "apolitical artist." He was having it both ways, of course: he received support from an unpopular government and publically distanced himself from connections to that government, thus infuriating both sides.

On his return from South America the newspaper columns were incensed, and it is clear that the scandal provoked by his statements in Argentina—even beyond every possible misinterpretation of them—fueled a sudden change in Pirandello's political attitudes. This change is best seen as a symptom, surfacing in unexpected circumstances and appearing as a crisis, with roots that were much deeper and far-reaching. The political uncertainties in which the author for a time wavered seemed to find in the trip to Argentina the occasion that led him involuntarily to question—albeit in cautious public statements—a political role with which he was not entirely comfortable. Although he felt obliged to make a decisive choice, Pirandello was aware that there was little way out of the situation. He constantly returned to this concern in his letters to Marta of 1928. The key reasons for his evolving political views, aside from the usual interpretations related to his tour of Argentina, are most likely to be found in the historical events during those months that would radically transform the life of the country.

In Italy, the months before the Teatro d'Arte's trip to Argentina witnessed the culmination of a political development that would persist for the next twenty years. Indeed, the years 1925-1926 witnessed the last gasps of what had remained of liberty. Through a mounting series of regulations, the regime consolidated its dictatorship over society. It is almost superfluous to recall the storm of legislation enacted to silence the few voices of journalistic opposition, to rein in local autonomy, and to penalize individuals who were not considered sufficiently loyal for public service—not to mention the total subjection of the judicial system and the suppression of independent labor unions.

Such was the social climate in the mid-20s, while the small and still fighting group of free voices was about to be snuffed out, especially after the imprisonment of the Communist party leader Antonio Gramsci (the party was outlawed in 1926) and the beating and death of Piero Gobetti, a prominent liberal journalist and intellectual. While this process of fascistization, which had by then reached an advanced stage, was being imposed with arrogant brutality, Pirandello was embarking for Argentina. Coincidentally, while Pirandello was leaving with the Teatro d'Arte, Mussolini had, just a few hours before, delivered his famous "Speech on the Ascension" (May 26, 1927), which became a reference point in Fascist doctrine, stating that opposition was unnecessary to healthy totalitarian systems like the fascist regime. Those were the last steps of Mussolini's march on Rome, which had begun five years before in 1922. It is worth noting here the almost positive use of the term *totalitarian*, a word which now has only negative connotations, but which had then only recently been coined and referred in a general way to the large modern states of 'total' social organization and control.

Going to the New World meant an escape from the dramatic tensions of the times, leaving behind a situation that was growing more oppressive each day. It also meant a chance to use the freedom of art to reckon with the meaning of freedom. Was it still the case that, outside the country, he would acknowledge himself to the world as a member of the party he had joined less than two years before?

Together with his concerns as an artist and theater director setting off for the stages of an unknown country, Pirandello must have harbored many uncertainties and questions, which he must have already had while living in an Italy imprisoned by a party that identified itself with the state. The resulting consolidated social order was one which had perhaps seduced the writer himself.

"Unspeakable things are happening"

A better understanding of Pirandello's thoughts on contemporary events can perhaps be gained through the letters he wrote to Marta at the time. Here we can glimpse the evolution of his ideas between 1926 and 1928, when he began to express new reservations about Mussolini and the ruling regime. In the early letters, when the Teatro d'Arte was in its heyday, there was still a strong sense of trust in state institutions. For example, on August 11, 1926, Pirandello wrote to Marta about the possibility of access to the Teatro Argentina:

> Meanwhile I can tell you that, following Mussolini's telephone call to the governor, today the matter of the Teatro Argentina is settled. Monday we will sign the contract, at 4 p.m. in the Campidoglio (U).

In letters written in 1928, however, we immediately sense a drastic change in Pirandello's attitude. Consider, for example, a letter of July 8, 1928, concerning a meeting called for the next day by Giuseppe Bottai, the state minister of corporations. Theater directors, agents, and critics had been invited to discuss the current crises in the theater world. Pirandello wrote to Marta of his intention to attend, but he expressed reservations that he could not believe wholeheartedly in the initiative:

> It is, however, useless, for the time being, to hope that any serious decision might be made. There will be the usual empty words. If the government really wants to do something for the theaters, it shouldn't consult anybody. It has consulted so many people so many times, and it has never done anything. If it keeps on consulting people who will never be able to agree with each other, because their interests are [opposed] opposite, it is a sign that it intends to put up a show of concern for the theater, but after all that it will still do nothing—and who knows for how long! (P, pp. 18-9).

Here it is evident that the writer did not hold out much trust in the government's intervention, and in this sort of partisan game he had identified the ambiguous strategy of Fascism, which habitually temporized in order to nourish hopes while rendering all the interested parties increasingly anemic, depriving them of all power of decision and counsel.

The next day Pirandello, confirming his predictions of the day before, wrote to Marta saying that the meeting with minister Bottai included "representatives of several artist unions, or so-called 'artist' unions." But nothing of substance had come of it. Besides this outcome, which he had predicted, Pirandello's words highlight the empty role of the now entirely compromised unions, which had in reality ceased to function with the law of April 3, 1926 suppressing the freedom of the unions and their right to strike. Pirandello, enraged by what he had heard, let all his bitterness erupt at the financial help that the government had promised earlier to those companies that showed the most signs of compliance.

From this point on, a desire to expatriate became a recurrent theme in his letters, culminating in his move to Germany in October 1928, which signaled the beginning of the author's voluntary exile. He repeatedly expressed in strong terms a desire to be independent of the morass of state affairs that had gripped the theater scene in Italy, and he held out to Marta high hopes that this freedom would come with success abroad. On July 12, 1928, he wrote that he could not wait to

> get away from this country where unspeakable things are happening, such that I cannot narrate by letter but which I'll tell you about in person in Genoa. I spoke at length about them with [Telesio] Interlandi, from whom I received this information; and more and more I've been confirmed in the idea of leaving my country—convinced as I am that for someone like me it is no longer possible to live in Italy. I'll return, if I ever return, when I no longer need anybody. In the meantime you should immediately get your passport renewed (P, p. 20).

In the next day's letter, he continued in the same tone about a journal that Interlandi wanted to start. He confessed that he had no faith in the undertaking because of everything he had heard and everything that Interlandi himself had told him. Yet again he referred to things that he could not write to her because they were absolutely "incredible," and could only be mentioned in person. They have "increased my horror toward my country and my first belief that, at least for the time being, life is not possible for me here. We must stay in Germany for at least one year...and put together a great fortune. Then we'll come back rich, independent of everyone, and be our own bosses" (P, p. 22).

What he was talking about specifically we cannot precisely know, and even Marta in later years could not recall. But we do know that the "incredible things" told him by his friend Interlandi ultimately reinforced his "horror" for his own country, where he says it is impossible to live (at that time Interlandi was managing editor of the Roman newspaper *Il*

Tevere, and later would became editor of *The Defense of the Race*, a racist and anti-Semitic propaganda vehicle whose publications in 1938 preceded the racial laws against Jews in Italy). But other indications in the letters do offer some hints as to his state of mind. A couple months later, on September 22, 1928, he wrote to Marta that Interlandi had been over for dinner and had spoken of the confusion everyone feels about the uncertainty of the current situation. Attempting to interpret the difficult moment, Pirandello sets out to explain the government's strategy, which had by then become much clearer to him:

> As soon as somebody gives any sign of achieving a preeminent position in any field—however diligently he might watch out and defend himself, being careful, with an eye on everything, ready to avoid traps and to foil plots—things start to happen in such a way that he himself will start to feel uncomfortable with any move he makes, at any step he takes, and he is thus obliged—being deprived of any support—to get back in line. For someone else, disparagements, vague accusations, or even open polemics immediately begin—starting, stopping, and starting all over again. For a third person, who already boasts of being sure of his influence and of having an acknowledged and recognized power, there is suddenly a flat denial, a definite setback that knocks him down into a most embarrassing position, and so on. The purpose of all this is to make sure that nobody gets his head up. Around Him [Mussolini], a level of heads reaching only to the knee, and not an inch higher. This way, everything remains forcibly low and confused, and there is really nothing left but mediocrity and confusion.... After chatting for three hours, I felt more and more discouraged, as if I could not even breathe anymore (P, p. 23).

He was reiterating more forcefully feelings that he had already harbored for at least several months. Earlier, on July 8, 1928, he had written in the same passionate vein:

We must definitely go away from Italy for some time, and come back only when we will not be dependent on anyone for anything, our own bosses. Here you will see nothing but everybody tearing each other to pieces, in public and privately, with the purpose of making it impossible for anybody to actually achieve something that everyone is shamelessly fighting for. Politics pervades everything. Slander, calumny, and intrigue are the weapons everybody is using. Life in Italy has become suffocating. Out! Out! Far! Far away! (P, p. 19).

A theatrical 'rivalry' with Mussolini

As mentioned already, in the middle of October, 1928, Pirandello left for Berlin, having convinced Marta, along with her sister Cele, to join him. But by the middle of March, 1929, Marta was back in Milan, having left Pirandello desperate and lovesick in Germany.

In light of the events of 1926-1928, the author's decision to leave Italy for Germany seems to be the result of a growing crisis, together with the progressive closing of cultural horizons into the narrow straits of an evermore stultifying nationalism, while the regime, now entirely in control, no longer had any limits on its arrogance. His departure was timely, since in December of 1928, just months after he left, the Fascist Grand Council became the supreme organ of political power. To be sure, his departure was not a true political exile, since he was not compelled but rather chose to leave the country. In fact, just a few months later (in March, 1929), he accepted a nomination to the newly created Italian Academy.

There were other professional reasons for him to go abroad, but without a doubt his sympathies for Fascism and for Mussolini had come to an end, and he was not at all pleased that this 'Romanized' Italy, with its menacing nationalism, had driven the country away from the rest of Europe. He surely must have sensed that every attack on freedom was fundamentally an attack on art as well, which was for him the only thing of real value. Even in Germany, however, he felt embattled as an artist. In a letter to Marta on June 1, 1930, after a production of *Tonight We Improvise* which he thought had been a disaster, he wrote: "This is Berlin. I felt as if I were in Italy. I don't know where I should go. Hatred follows me everywhere. Perhaps rightly so: I should go away from life, this way, chased away by the hatred of those triumphant cowards; by the incomprehension of the stupid majority" (P, p. 148).

It is worth recalling here Marta's own comments on this letter in her preface to the 1986 reissue of Nardelli's 1932 biography of Pirandello, *L'uomo segreto* [The Secret Man]: "He felt, therefore, as if he was on the other side of a cruel wall. 'Hatreds' had wounded him, these 'hatreds' had made him despise even some of his old friends." Perhaps among those who were considered among his "old friends," and whom Pirandello secretly despised, might have been Interlandi. "The tragedy of the *Mountain Giants*," she continued,

> which he had already conceived in 1928, when Pirandello gave a long interview to Bottazzi of "Corriere della Sera," (October 13, 1928) [just before he went to Germany] was a very clear allegory of the "central idea" that tormented him until his death in 1936. The world was regressing into barbarism and had become more and more incapable of understanding the real values of art, and was determined to eliminate them. The crude and unsophisticated "Giants" are unable to distinguish real facts from the fictions on stage (and they want to destroy those characters who they find unpleasant); but in Pirandello's mind, other less visible forms of spiritual coarseness are no less dangerous. That of the fanatic who wants to make art subservient to political ideology, but also that of those clever ones who with elastic conscience take advantage of art in order to create alliances, careers, money, power. In other words, he saw that the basic values of European civilization were in danger, which, by respecting those values, had achieved so much in the domain of the spirit (p. XI).

Marta's words confirm that Pirandello's change in attitude toward the regime had more profound roots that went beyond the single incident during the tour in South America. It was a crisis that surfaced gradually in different ways, but events and the letters show that Pirandello was perfectly aware of the uncertain political situation and how it was also having ramifications in the professional world of the arts. He was obviously worried about the danger of being forced to descend, for his profession's sake, into ever more indecorous compromises, which his free spirit would not allow him to accept. Above all, he was concerned about making art subservient to political ideology.

The hatreds that wounded Pirandello were also aimed at Marta. As she wrote in this same preface: "I believe I cannot remain silent here, that the unfair war and the hatreds against Pirandello extended also against myself—and with a ruthlessness that still offends me. To tell the truth, it opened an opportunity for me to abandon the Maestro and his works, when Suvini and Zerboni [the dominant theatrical agency] proposed setting up a company that would only stage plays to which they held the rights. I turned them down without reservation. When they saw my tenacious fidelity, in order to obstruct Pirandello's theater from that time, many of them have found it useful to obstruct and fight against me as well" (p. XII).

The word "hatred," which Marta uses repeatedly here, is also not uncommon in Pirandello's own vocabulary: "the hatred of triumphant cowards," as he said in his letter of June 1, 1930. Perhaps these hatreds were not only the result of his attitude toward the Fascist regime, but also of his request for the institution of state theaters, which would have wrested control from the despicable machinations of politicians. Although the idea was a good one from a social point of view, it was probably considered too revolutionary according to the paternalistic spirit of the time. Or perhaps it was his success itself, which had made Pirandello a national treasure, that could have created jealousies, even on the part of Mussolini himself.

It is not widely known that Mussolini, besides his dreams of political power, also nurtured literary and theatrical ambitions. He had been passionate about theater since his youth, when he would scribble ideas for future plays and draft scenes and monologues that he left unfinished. These literary diversions accompanied him through youth into maturity. In this regard his 'artistic' encounter with Giovacchino Forzano in the summer of 1929 was decisive, when the two undertook a theatrical collaboration. Mussolini reserved the creative role for himself, and Forzano took the role of writer. The first fruit of this collaboration was the tragedy *Campo di maggio (May's Field)*, which describes the last days of Napoleon. It was performed at the Argentina Theater in Rome on December 18, 1930. Mussolini and his family sat in the most prominent box, above members of government, party officials, and the crème de la crème of the Roman aristocracy all seated below. It was greeted with resounding success: the actors and the author were called back for an astonishing twenty-five encores (Forzano was listed on the marquee; Mussolini had the good sense not to put his own name). But in its triumphal tour the historical drama was listed as the work of Benito Mussolini and Giovacchino Forzano.

Villafranca followed in 1932. Performed at the Teatro Lirico in Milan, the play focused on the events of armistice and peace that followed the second war of Italian Independence in 1859. It exalted the sacrifice of the people, who even when suffering injustice or hardship must never give up. Their third and last work, *Cesare*, was performed at Rome's Teatro Argentina in 1939. Despite the ambitiousness of the production, the show was a flop. What most disappointed the audience, it seems, was that the play's climax, the assassination of Caesar, was not represented on stage at all (as it is in Shakespeare), but is merely reported by a messenger to a group of peaceful colonists embarking for Africa. This element was a blatant reference to Italy's colonial adventures in East Africa. On second thought, however, perhaps representing the death of the dictator on stage would have been, for Mussolini, a little too close for comfort.

It is possible then that during Mussolini's years as a 'playwright,' Pirandello's outstanding presence on the Italian theater scene was not entirely to the dictator's liking. On the other hand, he was most likely aware that it would not have been easy to silence or impede Pirandello's great talents, or to obstruct the fame he had achieved abroad. He could, however, create difficulties for him and obstacles to his art in Italy. Circumstances and moods could change at any moment, and Mussolini the great patron could suddenly become an enemy. Such shifts in mood are apparent when we compare statements made in the letters over the span of years in question. Some of Pirandello's letters of 1926 and, later, of 1928, which we cited above, attest to this souring of relations between Mussolini and the state, on the one hand, and Pirandello on the other.

In this regard, Mussolini's own pronouncements about the 'crisis' in the theater world, during a rally in Rome for playwrights on April 28, 1933, take on greater meaning. His speech on this occasion stressed that theater should be accessible to the masses, that theatrical works must have wide appeal, and that they must stir up strong common feelings. At the same time, he directed playwrights to stop dramatizing the love triangle, saying that the world had enough of such plays and its time was now finished. Besides the fact that he was calling into question at least half of all comedies and tragedies throughout history, this also could be read as a more or less direct attack against Pirandello himself, whose plays, after all, though deeply rooted in traditional dramatic canons, were all innovative and revolutionary takes on that same triangle—and for this he had achieved his worldwide fame.

Mussolini was not Pirandello's only dramatic 'rival' from within the government rank and file of the time. We must also recall that Telesio Interlandi himself, and Corrado Pavolini, who were both very close to the dictator and active in the government, entertained theatrical ambitions. Together the two wrote *La croce del Sud*, a mediocre play that Pirandello included in the repertoire of the Teatro d'Arte during the tour of Argentina in 1927. The critics demolished the play when it was performed. It is clear that these were exceedingly complex relationships, in which the mutual relations and ambitions of each complicated matters all the more. Dramatists endorsed by Mussolini well understood that any artistic comparison with Pirandello would have been to their disadvantage, even while they knew that with their political power they were the strongest. By the end of the 1920s, the Fascist regime had already positioned all of its men in the right places, and it was precisely this ambiguous position of artistic inferiority and great political advantage that provoked the tensions that would convince Pirandello to quit the field.

Marta appeals to Il Duce

Pirandello's uncertain relationship with Marta Abba also played an important role in his decision to move to Germany. As motivations, there were several work opportunities that looked very promising for both of them. In a letter from the summer of 1928, after a conversation with Bernstiel (an agent for the German film company Ufa), Pirandello wrote: "He offered me the following: a six-month position as artistic director, with a monthly salary of 6,000 Marks, equal to 27,000 Lira, three subjects for films—in which You will have the leading role, with a separate contract—for which I'll receive 15,000 Marks and 10% on gross profits" (Rome, July 4, 1928; L, p. 31).

Moreover, he predicted for both of them more favorable work conditions, and for the actress certain success, one of the enticements that had convinced her to join him in Berlin. But failing in his attempt to find new work opportunities for himself and Marta abroad, and with Marta back in Italy after only six months, in later letters Pirandello changed the negative tone he had used in the months before leaving Italy, returning to a more cautious position. It seems that he had been informed of the possibility that Mussolini wanted to offer support to create a number of state theaters. In the letters following Marta's departure, more conciliatory attitudes emerged toward all that he had fled from a few months earlier—even some hints of a kind of new trust of Mussolini.

It should be emphasized that very often his reservations are directed more at the Fascist system and those exercising power rather than at Mussolini himself, in whom, despite some human weakness, he recognized certain merits. He was convinced that "the state theaters will be set up the way I want them, because Mussolini always keeps his promises. We must learn to wait, because he needs time; woe unto those who get tired of waiting" (Berlin, March 26, 1929; P, pp. 45-6). Later that year, still believing in the project, he wrote to Marta, "I'll go to Rome to renew the battle; I'll make every possible effort to speak to Mussolini about establishing the regional theaters. I must somehow find the energy for it" (Milan, December 12, 1929; P, p. 99). Although Mussolini did not keep his promise, for several years Pirandello hoped that the project of state/regional theaters would materialize. By reading between the lines, we get the sense that Pirandello, having failed Marta in Berlin, is trying to present Mussolini's patronage of the state theaters as a new opportunity for the actress (with himself), whose career had once more been cast into uncertainty.

In fact, Marta herself later turned to Mussolini because of her difficulties. Her first contact with the Duce took place in February, 1932, after she returned to Italy from Paris, where she had been performing a French version of Pirandello's *Man, Beast and Virtue*, to critical and popular acclaim. Encouraged by her achievements abroad, she decided to pay homage to the head of state, and to take the occasion to speak with him as well about the difficult working situation in Italy. In a letter of February 4, 1932, she tells Pirandello the results of this meeting:

> Here I am, the next day after the meeting…I couldn't sleep last night, thinking of all the things I could have said but didn't, and thinking of my impressions of that tragic man…. The meeting had been set, by telegram, for 6pm, then it was postponed until 6:30, and finally I was admitted into his office at 7. The meeting lasted, I believe, about half an hour. He asked me about the plays, and how many performances I had done, and even how much I had earned. I right away raised the subject of my past frustrations and he asked me the reasons. He knew everything from the press…I understand, in short, that the people who surround him, and the absence of those

who could provide him with accurate information, has been very harmful. He only knows what they are willing to tell him. The conversation turned to you. He said that you have a foul temper. "I have bestowed on him all those honors, because I consider him a genius. But he has a foul temper." Also the commemoration you gave at the Academy in honor of Verga, it was not appreciated. Your attack on d'Annunzio was not appreciated. And it was at the least inappropriate. About all this, Maestro, unfortunately you know how I feel, and I can't say I disagree with him. You, Great among Greats, should have been more generous, and not say things that bothered even those who are against d'Annunzio. Then he asked me what my plans were. I told him that I would reorganize a theatrical company in September. "Ah, only in September?" And if I would expand my repertoire. I told him I had already expanded it: Molnar, [Heinrich] Mann, and he expressed his reservations about Mann, who perhaps doesn't please him. Well, in conclusion, when I understood how much he had been surrounded and changed, I felt like crying. I said to him: "It's the same old story, etc...on one side are the noble and pure...on the other..." He seemed to become a bit pensive when I spoke about the laws in other countries that prohibit owners of rights on plays to also run companies etc. etc.

In conclusion, I am and feel, although he treated me with great courtesy, almost discouraged because I did not try to move him with my live voice, discouraged that some word, a pledge of faith, that I expected never came. Are the others right? Do I not perhaps need to leave and abandon the game? I don't know, I don't anything anymore...(C, pp. 236-7).

How provocative to read Marta relaying Mussolini's own impressions of him! In fact, there is another interesting independent witness of

Mussolini's thinking about Pirandello at the time. Between March 23 and April 4, 1932, the German-Jewish journalist Emil Ludwig had a series of conversations with Mussolini, published that same year as *Colloqui con Mussolini* [Talks with Mussolini, 1933]. The Italian dictator discussed many topics—including his thoughts on Jews and anti-Semitism: "Anti-Semitism doesn't exist in Italy" (p. 70), he says at one point; and on feminism and the women's suffrage movement: "Woman must play a passive part ... My notion of woman's role in the state is utterly opposed to feminism. Of course I do not want women to be slaves, but if here in Italy I proposed to give our women votes, they would laugh me to scorn. As far as political life is concerned, they do not count here" (p. 170). Finally he turns to questions of art. Discussing modern drama, Mussolini states: "among d'Annunzio's plays. The two I like the best are *La figlia di Jorio* and *La fiaccola sotto il moggio*. I am a great admirer of Shaw, but sometimes find his freakishness annoying. Pirandello writes Fascist plays without meaning to do so! He shows that the world is what we wish to make it, that it is our creation" (p. 214). However one looks at it, this interpretive appropriation of Pirandello's aesthetics as the very definition of Fascism is quite striking. If nothing else, it is perhaps a sign of Pirandello's international celebrity that makes it desirable for Mussolini to label him and his art as quintessentially Fascist.

There is also a draft of a letter that Pirandello wrote, with no date (though it was probably written in 1933, after a previous letter that Marta had written to Mussolini), which Marta was to copy and send under her name to Mussolini. She wanted to request a meeting with him to discuss new regulations for theatrical companies the Fascist government was enacting. She felt that the government was making it more difficult for theater companies to operate. She (and Pirandello) were again concerned about the Fascist "Trust" system, which would systematically shut out independent theater workers. Written in Pirandello's own hand, it says:

> Duce, through the benevolence Your Excellence has honored
> me with, and the gratitude that makes me indebted to You

from the depths of my heart, I feel the duty to inform you of what I have done and achieved since that day I came to Rome, after concluding my tour with the Company, to organize the ways and means of setting in order my future artistic activities (U).

In the rest of the draft Pirandello relates to Mussolini—in Marta's voice—meetings she held with a cultural minister at the time, and her dissatisfaction and concerns about a plan for theater funding that seemed only to be to the further advantage of the existing theater monopoly, and not in any way assisting independent actors and theater workers. The draft, written on letterhead from the Excelsior Hotel in Rome, remains unfinished, and on it Marta had later noted in red: "original draft of letter written in the Maestro's hand that I had to write to the Duce. I don't remember if I sent it, the letter appears to be unfinished."

As has been said, from 1929 to 1934 the actress had her own company organized with the financial help of her father, who invested most of his fortune in the company. To clarify the meaning of the letter, Marta explained to me how difficult those years were for her, as she was solely responsible for a company that was always in a precarious financial state. There were also disappointments with the theatrical world, in which a single bad review in a local paper would be enough to turn the public away from a production. The idea of writing to Mussolini to ask him to help her was suggested by Rosetta (Rosa Teodorani Mussolini), the daughter of Arnoldo, Mussolini's brother, who was a great fan of Marta and later became a close friend.

As Pirandello had promised in the above-mentioned letter written to Marta on December 12, 1929, over the years he paid several visits to the Duce about state/regional theaters and other matters. Corrado Alvaro recalls in his preface to Pirandello's *Novelle per un anno* that, leaving after one of these meetings at Palazzo Venezia in Rome, Pirandello told Ugo Ojetti, a prominent journalist, "He [Mussolini] is a vulgar man," and recounted how Mussolini, in reference to his fame, had reproved him for his timidity and modesty. Pirandello had called to his attention that timidity is a form of respect. Il Duce shot back: "But never with women!

When one loves a woman, he gets to the point and throws her on the couch!" Pirandello was justifiably scandalized, not only because what Mussolini had said offended his own deep respect for women, but also because of the possible innuendo it may have contained about his own gossip-ridden relationship with Marta.

Pirandello must also have thought of Mussolini's own notorious behavior, whose active romantic affairs—with extramarital mistresses and many casual relations—were open secrets, among which was his 19-year relationship with Margherita Sarfatti, or his more recent young mistress Claretta Petacci, with whom, after abandoning Sarfatti in 1932, he started a new relationship. This courageous girl loved "Ben" (as she always called him) up to the last days of his life, and tried to make him happy although she was aware that he was unfaithful. For years everybody knew that Claretta would be brought to Palazzo Venezia almost everyday in a sidecar entering by a side entrance, and would wait for hours in the Hall of the Zodiac—at five an assistant would bring her tea—for Mussolini to come whenever he had time to spend with her. She was completely devoted to him, and decided to join Mussolini in the last months of his life, refusing to embark on the plane that would have carried her safely to Spain. She spent her last night with him in a country house before they were shot by a group of anti-Fascist Partisans.

Artists, Theater, and the State

As we can see, the careers of both Marta and Pirandello were constantly intertwined with the political life of the regime. To Pirandello, however, it was always a distraction and annoyance, lost as he was in his dream of a pure art, tormented and exalted by his obsessive infatuation with Marta, and preoccupied with his own troubles, namely his wife's mental illness and the ever-present burden of supporting his three children and their families. After this long period of pain and unhappiness, Marta Abba appeared and erased the past, and it is in his letters to her that he reveals his psycho-physical suffering, the incomprehension and dishonesty of others, and the feeling of solitude which compels him to want always to be elsewhere. As he once wrote to Marta:

> For all my forty years of labor, which has made me a great deal of money, I have nothing left; other people always took it, it has served other people's interests; I still want to keep on working, always working, because I know that I do not know how to do anything else. I don't know why it is that now they do not want my work to bring in as much money as before; if it did, it would continue to make money for other people and not for me, because I never enjoyed my money, I never knew what to do with it for myself, it has always been used by me to make other people happy; my only unhappiness now is that I cannot make other people as happy as I could before or even more so (Berlin, April 11, 1929; P, pp. 66-7).

These pressing problems made it difficult for him to be engaged politically. For Pirandello the political question was limited to the potential for theater; otherwise he saw bureaucracy and obscure favoritism for others who were willing to be subservient to the state but who did not truly care about artistic liberty. In this regard, something Marta recalled to me in a conversation in the spring of 1984 seems to the point:

> The negotiations to obtain the theaters were always long and uncertain; sometimes we had difficulties getting good theaters. The conditions discussed were always changed when the contract was written. Difficulties always arose that nobody could predict. There were also questions about the repertoire; often agents requested that we perform five different plays in a very short run. It was an unbearably tiring life. For example, it was very difficult to get the theaters in Milan, often because of the inexperience of the agent, who was incapable of making the theater owners understand that to attract audiences we

would have to play certain plays more than others; also because of the theater owners' personal interests, they would want me to perform shoddy little plays, simply because they owned rights to them. But sometimes even when I performed the plays that belonged to them, there would be still other difficulties.

Ultimately, Pirandello was trying to do his own work, and avoided getting directly involved in political issues. He was aware that there were many risks, although he was convinced that political support could have made his own journey easier. There was nothing to do, therefore, in the political world for a writer who was used to representing on stage repressions and complexes that were not derived from power, but were rather existential, in which men find themselves in conflicting positions, in a state of transgression even as it is normalized by institutions. What could Pirandello possibly offer to the ideology of Fascism? Perhaps only the conventions of an existential mechanism as the playing field between fiction and reality. If anything, the most revolutionary aspect of his message is the form in which the content is presented, and which shakes from the depths the rules of the theater.

In the letters and all of his writings, however, we rarely see any intention to use the theater as a political soapbox (his most political play *The New Colony* being an obvious exception). Rather, it is clear that the theater is always the center of his existential conflict. The ambitions of certain characters whom Pirandello confined in a dull conformity of modest but secure activity, often engaged obsessively in bureaucratic duties, did not much bother the censors. Being themselves exactly these sorts of low-level bureaucratic functionaries, and true to character, they kept themselves occupied trying to suppress those whose opposition to the state was open and unambiguous.

Chapter 3

THE HAND THAT TURNS THE CRANK

"What most interests me about America is the birth of new life forms. Life, under the pressure of natural and social necessities, seeks out and finds these new forms there. Watching them come into being is an incomparable joy to the spirit" (Luigi Pirandello, *Corriere della Sera*, 1929).

More than ten years had passed since the legendary date of December 28, 1895, when the Lumière brothers had presented a movie show in Paris consisting of ten of their short films, thus giving birth to the motion picture as a popular spectacle (earlier shows had been more exhibitions of technology than true entertainment). Films had grown in scale. They made ever greater artistic claims for themselves and borrowed more and more from literature, history and the theater. After the first notices and proclamations concerning the motion picture had appeared between the first and the second decades of the century, film had fully entered the life of some writers and intellectuals. Attracted more by the worldly atmosphere and the prospect of easy gains than by artistic motives, many writers were tentative in their approach to this new form of entertainment. During the second decade of the century, the motion picture began to garner more and more public attention. As cinema grew more popular a faithful public began to take shape, along with a specialized journalistic criticism, a separate literature, and interests that caught up not only political, religious and economic institutions but intellectuals as well. Europe was in a general ferment over film: unexpected conflicts and contrasts of opinion opened the debate, which revolved as much around the roles of art in this new type of entertainment as around the new medium's semantic value.

The debate flourished widely in France, Great Britain, Austria, Germany, and Russia. In Russia, for example, Leo Tolstoy proclaimed himself favorably impressed with the new invention in 1908, while five years later the Futurist poet and playwright Vladimir Mayakovsky denied its artistic value. In 1913 George Lukács published his "Thoughts on Film Aesthetics" (*Frankfurter Zeitung*, October 10, 1913), as other writers and intellectuals continued to express their opinions on the subject: Max Brod, Peter Altenberg, Hugo von Hofmannsthal, and later G. K. Chesterton and Jean Cocteau. Cinema was interpreted above all in relation to theater and literature, and it seemed especially to threaten the craftsmen in these older media. For its peculiar ability to flesh out literary and dramatic texts and historical events, more and more authors and artists began to embrace the cinematic experience.

Because of his idiosyncratic view of existence, Pirandello's own literary treatment of cinema was much more nuanced than simple celebration, and was thus perfectly attuned to the prevailing mood of ambivalence about film. His relation to film was complex, and his literary development, moving from verse to narrative to theater, parallels the rise of cinematic art and the film industry. His interest in new forms of expression naturally drew him to film, which always fascinated him and fired his imagination. During the second decade of the twentieth century he was deeply involved in the film industry, writing screenplays and associating closely with leading players in Italian film. In the twenties and thirties he would even expand his circle of contacts to include key figures in German, British, and American movie-making.

In 1915, Pirandello's interest in film led him to write *Action!*, a novel that constitutes his first theoretical statement on the new world created by film technology. It brought together in a compelling narrative form all that Pirandello was then thinking about the art of film, and was a major artistic contribution to the wider discussion of cinema at that time. Published in installments in the *Nuova Antologia* from June through August of 1915,

Action! was republished ten years later in Florence as *The Notebooks of Serafino Gubbio, Cameraman*. Through the novel's main character Pirandello expresses and explores the crises of contemporary man, who is obliged to face and to reckon with a technological world that impinges on every aspect of his life. In a life determined by technological forces, Serafino, a cameraman at the "Kosmograph" production company, witnesses through the camera's lens the fragmentation of human beings and the consequent estrangement of humankind from natural feelings and behavior. In the end this annuls his very being. Indeed, with extreme self-control he finds himself filming not a fictional scene but a tragically real drama, when the actor Aldo Nuti, in a fit of jealousy, kills the Russian actress Vania Nestoroff, and is then mauled by the tiger that he was supposed to shoot down. Seeing no way out, Serafino goes mute from shock and becomes entirely uncommunicative, losing his only means of expressing himself—his voice.

On the one hand, Serafino identifies himself for professional reasons with the hand that turns the camera crank, as if he is a mere part of the movie camera. On the other hand, in the act of narrating the story he recovers his humanity and destroys the unfeeling mechanism that had previously trapped him. Clearly Pirandello was exploring, through Serafino Gubbio, the theme of mechanical modernity, which is defined by technology's tortured new relations to humankind, and somehow aligns himself with the exaltation of the machine that was such a favored theme in the days of the Futurists. *The Notebooks of Serafino Gubbio, Cameraman* was thus an important early literary response to the new artistic and technological mode of cinematic representation, which seemed to transform theatrical productions into mass-produced market commodities. For Pirandello regarded cinema not simply as a novel artistic medium but as a new product of and a tool for consumerism. In the novel it is described as monstrous, and becomes a metaphor for more sinister forces, expressed in a symbolic way by the enormous black spider to which the camera's tripod is frequently likened: "on its knock-kneed tripod a huge spider watching for its prey, a spider that sucks in and absorbs their live reality to render it up an evanescent, momentary appearance, the play of a mechanical illusion in the eyes of the public" (*Notebooks*, p. 106). And Serafino becomes the man who feeds the spider: "the beastlinesses that I have to serve up all day long as food for this black spider on its tripod, which eats and is never filled, I do not speak of them... all the people who are driven by necessity to feed this machine upon their own modesty, their own dignity, I do not speak of them...." (p. 141).

Pirandello's ironic ambivalence toward film leads him in *Action!* to portray screenwriters and actors who participate reluctantly in filmmaking mainly because the pay is good, and therefore cannot or are not inclined openly to express contempt for that terrible little machine that drains their souls dry, like a spider does its victims, rendering them back in the small rolls of processed celluloid film. This final 'product' represents the degradation of their personality, distancing them from a more lively contact with the public. These deadening and distancing effects of films are why Serafino Gubbio comes to feel less like a real person than merely a hand that turns the crank. The criticisms that Pirandello seems to level here are directed less at the new medium of expression itself than at the particular cultural forms that were developing around the use of film and that seemed to be working to subjugate film and its artistic processes to the creation of yet another degraded product for popular consumption. It offered the promise of satisfying the public thirst for stage representations through mechanical reproduction, which could very well short-circuit the traditional theatrical and dramatic world entirely.

It is almost as if there were two—perhaps even three—Pirandellos when it came to cinema. One was very excited by the new horizons opened by film. Another was frightened by the threats it posed to the world of theater and to humanity itself. Yet another considered these threats in a more positive light—as a possibility to widen enormously the audience for theatrical shows, and also to turn greater profits from the expanded audience.

Writing on January 25, 1918 to the film director Anton Giulio Bragaglia, who had asked him for the subject of a film, Pirandello proposed *Action!*, which he thought would make a truly original film, since it was based upon a 'movie within a movie.' We see that the problem of acting as a mirror of human actions, as well as a source of what it sometimes reflects, has already emerged as a metaphor in Pirandello's cinematic thought, as it would later in his dramatic conceptions (figuring as a critical theme in *Six Characters* three years later, and in the form of a 'play within a play' that permeates the so-called "theater trilogy" that included *To Each His Own* and *Tonight We Improvise*).

In this self-reflexive exploration of film's more complex relations to 'real' life, *Action!* can be seen as an early anticipation of a theme that has become relatively popular in recent films, which are beginning to explore more creatively the early social and cultural history of filmmaking. For example, in the 2000 release *Shadow of a Vampire*, John Malkovich plays the part of the early twentieth-century filmmaker F.W. Murnau in a story about the making of the now classic film version of Bram Stoker's *Dracula*, *Nosferatu* (1922). The film plays with the possibility that real vampirism had been filmed for the movie, though unsuspected by the filmmakers as it was happening. In this way the supposedly fictional world of the staged horror film is undercut by the gruesome realities discovered in the real Romania where they are on location to film the movie. Similarly, the 2003 made-for-TV picture, *Starring Pancho Villa as Himself*, tells the story — "based on true events" — of how Mexican revolutionary Pancho Villa (played by Antonio Banderas) called in American filmmakers to document his revolution on film, which he intended to be used for propaganda purposes in gaining support for his cause north of the border. Again, the movie explores the murky frontiers between what is 'real' and what is 'fiction' when a camera is rolling, and how the processes and industry of filmmaking have both opened new cultural possibilities and complicated human affairs and relations in surprising new ways. Such early twenty-first century films indicate a relatively intelligent attempt by moviemakers to explore their art's own history and the power and nature of their medium. At the turn of the last century, with film entering its first heyday, Pirandello was already undertaking similar, more prophetic explorations in *Action!*.

With this first novel on a cinematographic theme, Pirandello's tortured relationship with film, despite his continued reservations about it over the course of twenty years, entered powerfully into his multifaceted literary activity, which actually culminated with film, in the form of a last desperate attempt to bring to life a film version of the *Six Characters*. Throughout this long personal struggle, which had both creative and practical dimensions, his correspondence with Marta Abba was an important outlet for expressing his frustrations, visions, aspirations and setbacks. Thus the letters are a crucial source for our understanding of this stage in his career. In particular, like all those in and around the filmmaking industry, Pirandello had to deal with the radical technical revolution entailed by the shift from silent to sound pictures. And like many others who had found unique creative niches for themselves in silent films (Charlie Chaplin and Buster Keaton, for example) Pirandello's experiences with this shift were not entirely positive.

Despite his reservations, then, Pirandello's interests in cinema were therefore neither casual nor circumstantial. On the contrary, we can speak of a love-hate relationship that saw periods of enthusiasm give way to criticism and resentment, which were often generated by specific experiences with powerful figures and forces in the film industry itself. However, his ideas on film were also the result of thoughts that discerned in this new form of entertainment aesthetic and expressive possibilities all its own. It would be hard otherwise to explain his lengthy digressions on the subject during the last twenty years of his life in articles, letters, and interviews. Based on his theatrical experience, Pirandello developed and expressed keen interest in the technical and artistic characteristics of cinema, which encouraged him to explore new imaginative representations of subjects he had already treated in other mediums. Pirandello thought that depicting reality through moving visual forms might enhance, through images and wordless music, the medium of the theater. This art form, dubbed *cinemalografia* at the time, would harmonize the movement of scenes with musical scores. Pirandello was deeply convinced that this was his own original idea. When he found to his chagrin that others were thinking along similar lines, and even developing the idea, he felt that a creative vision rightfully his had been stolen from him.

The conflict between the static scene of the theater, designed for events which the dialogue helps to conjure up, and Pirandello's desire to see the representation of human emotions on the screen through images and music, took on profound significance for him. The plethora of possibilities allowed him to construct a perspective that served to highlight this new, audiovisual side to his talent. He had grasped the importance of film, though he brought with him all of the inflexibilities and prejudices which dramatic habits had imposed on him. What matters here are not the results Pirandello achieved in film—these were relatively scant—but rather his own will to engage with a new experience to which he believed he had something to offer. It was especially after the publication of *Action!* that Pirandello began his concerted and steady collaboration with screenwriters and film directors. He was very pleased that several of his short stories became the basis for screenplays that were produced as films, and he was thus able to begin to witness the cinematic potential of his stories. From this point forward, this fact would continue to exert influence on his literary imagination. These films included Augusto Genina's *Lo scaldino* (1919), Mario Gargiulo's *Lumie di Sicilia* (1919), Ugo Gracci's *Il lume dell'altra casa* (1920), Augusto Camerini's *Ma non e` una cosa seria* (1921), and Gennaro Righelli's *Il Viaggio* (1921). Although mostly forgotten now, these short films were modestly popular, if ephemeral, productions of the small-scale Italian film industry of the time.

Yet, like other Italian and European intellectuals during the decade, Pirandello also feared the total replacement of theater by film. This concern, which he showed to some degree even during the years of silent film, deepened with the advent of the talkie at the end of the 1920s. Pirandello realized the importance and implications of the sound motion picture, and was anxious about its effects on the theater (which, as usual, was generally considered by intellectuals and theatrical professionals to be on the threshold of a crisis). Yet he was also convinced that a newly sophisticated cinema incorporating sound could be turned to his artistic purposes. He believed, quite understandably, that the role of producing screenplays for the talkies should rightfully fall to playwrights, and acting to the theatrical professionals. He wrote in this vein to Marta Abba from Berlin:

> The whole world of the movies is going through a revolution. It looks as if the talking film is really a prodigy: they have succeeded in reproducing to perfection the human voice—close up, distant, tuned in all possible ways. Which means that they'll definitely need actors who know how to speak well, and therefore also playwrights who know how to make the characters of the no-longer-silent movies speak. You understand: if the characters of the film from now on are going to speak, not just anybody will be able to make them speak; it will be necessary to employ a writer who knows the art of the dramatic or comic dialogue—a theater writer. They will have to hire the best ones available" (Berlin, April 6, 1929; P, p. 62).

Worried by the overwhelming enthusiasm for film apparent in Germany, in the same letter to the actress he wrote passionately:

> "They affirm, however, with unbearable arrogance, that the legitimate theater is dead and buried; that soon nobody will care about it, because from now on there will be the talking film, which not only will reproduce the voices, but also will do things that the stage has never dreamed of doing" (pp. 62-63).

Although he was aware of the dangers and potentially catastrophic effects that film might have on theater, especially now that sound allowed film a far greater expressive range, theater continued for better or worse to be the primary source of Pirandello's professional and economic welfare. He was naturally attracted, however, by the possibilities that seemed open to the 'best' writers, among which he obviously considered himself. This would also have meant the transfer to the screen of the countless plots for short stories, novels and plays that poured continually from his typewriter. He was encouraged in his hopes by the prevailing atmosphere of cosmopolitanism and by the clear tendency of artists and journals, as the twenties gave way to the thirties, to favor artistic transfers between media.

Still, at this critical juncture Pirandello had to confront the inevitable problem that talking films faced if they were to be successfully internationalized: the language barrier. As usual, Pirandello confided his worries to Marta Abba:

> The English actors will not be able to speak anything but English; the Germans, German; the French actors, French; the Italians, Italian; neither is it possible to resort to translations, because the same actors will not be able to pronounce well the words translated into a language that is foreign to them. There will therefore no longer be any such thing as an international film, but instead English, German, French, Italian films, with significant reduction of the area of distribution, which has hitherto permitted the expenditure of enormous amounts of money for the production of every film. I don't know how well they will solve this problem, which involves not only the language, but also the financial aspect. Right now they are all crazy about the miraculous novelty of the "film that speaks" [Pirandello writes this phrase in English!]; not only in England are they as if possessed, but also in Germany, because they expect that it will soon speak German; but when it does speak *in German,* how will it be understood by the Americans and by the English people, and vice versa? They don't think about it (Berlin, April 6, 1929; P, p. 62).

On the one hand, then, is the old fear that had been felt ever since the first stirrings of silent film, and which is now made more acute by the arrival of sound film: that theater might be finally replaced by the new medium. On the other hand, Pirandello was also tempted to seek new outlets for his writing activity in talking films, although he realized they were inherently limited in the use of language on the international level. This view, which is not without contradictions, probably contributed to Pirandello's idea that film, unlike theater, should consist of the fusion of images and music. He was thinking not only of consciously 'cinematic' music, but also of already existing scores, with the aid of which moving images would take shape. The history of film and its soundtracks has shown that music composed in distant centuries can be adapted even for stories set in contemporary times, thanks to the flexibility of sounds in relation to images and words. The astonishing symbolic polyvalence of music was intensely suggestive to Pirandello as well, as it was to many others in a period so rich in cinematic technical innovations. He dreamed particularly of creating a context of images for the scores; already captivated by his own idea in July of 1928, in a letter from Rome he expounded to Marta Abba his monumental project for the cinematic realization of the nine symphonies of Beethoven:

> [...] the way will be open to Germany for great things and great fortunes. And I am most happy, Marta, for You. I am thinking of nothing else. I have bought so many books in Rome: on Beethoven, for the idea You know about; and I am lagging in the reading of them. Magnificent visions, and things one has never seen are on their way" (July 6, 1928; L, pp. 36-7).

Ever the visionary, he foretold untold novelties springing from his imagination; always thinking of Marta, he imagines she will be the chief beneficiary of and collaborator in his creative gifts to the world. On the same subject a few days later, he wrote:

> I have again begun reading about Beethoven's life and the Nine Symphonies to get ready for the work You know about. It seems to me they will come off superbly. But I need the inspiration of the music. I will need to try to hear the symphonies again, one by one, somehow, carefully. Maybe I can find some nice little gramophone. The reading meanwhile of these books is giving me the right frame of mind and a sense of the spiritual mood of the musician at various points during his composition (Nettuno [Rome], July 10, 1928; L, p. 42).

Silly Symphonies

Pirandello, working tirelessly to generate these early cinematographic ideas, was now convinced of their originality. In a later letter from Berlin to Marta Abba, he tells her that he has already suggested the idea of a film incorporating music to Felix Bloch-Erben:

> Felix Bloch-Erben, in whose hands I put my idea for the musical film, will work to find, either in America or here, somebody who will want to realize it and invest millions. We must get started now, because it seems to me that so far the only way to solve the problem of internationalization is simply by making *sound* films. Sound—and not talking—films. The image, like music, can be understood by everybody; the word, no, because it is only in the language of those who speak it. But a representative of Tonfilm of England, with whom Bloch-Erben spoke today, said that my idea seemed brilliant, but only for a few selected people (as usual!) and not for the masses. "Pirandello [sic] is an exceptional poet [...]" (Berlin, April 6, 1929; P, p. 63).

It is clear that in making these considerations Pirandello could not rely either on subtitled translations or on techniques of dubbing, which were not yet in use, but which would soon allow an adequate solution to the problem of internationalization, and therefore of the diffusion of sound films. A symptom of the complexity created by the transition from silent to sound movies was a frustrating episode Pirandello himself experienced, and it exemplified the difficulties an author could face. A screenplay for a silent film might become unusable as soon as it was finished, since in the meantime the market, suddenly turned upside down by the novelty of sound, was clamoring for screenplays for the talkie. So striking a change inevitably led to tensions and misunderstandings between members of the profession.

In the spring of 1929 Pirandello, having settled for a few months in Germany, had just finished the screenplay of *Six Characters* commissioned by the producer and director Richard Eichberg (1888-1953). Adolf Lantz was then in the process of translating the play into German, and Pirandello found himself in a paradoxical situation with no clear solution, reminiscent of the kind that often befalls his own characters:

> I'm not leaving for London if I don't first obtain payment for the remaining several thousand marks Eichberg still owes me: five thousand. Do you realize what is going on? I am in this situation: between Eichberg who does not want to pay me before Lantz finishes the screenplay; and Lantz who does not want to finish translating it because he says that Eichberg wants to have the satisfaction of seeing him finish it so he can then say that as it is, he doesn't know what to do with it, since by order of the *British International*, he has to turn it into a sound film. Now, my contract with Eichberg mentions a silent film, not a talking film; therefore he cannot expect from me a talking film; and in fact, he does not expect this (Berlin, April 12, 1929; L, p. 127).

Ironically, Pirandello found himself caught in a characteristically Pirandellian situation: by sheer coincidence he happened to be completing a contracted work for a silent film screenplay at exactly the time when the industry was undergoing its revolution in sound, rendering his work in the old medium obsolete! The irony was not lost on the author, though surely he could not have found it very amusing.

Pirandello, at Eichberg's invitation, was ready not only to go to London to see the new talking films, among which was certainly *The Jazz Singer*, but also to "introduce words" into extant screenplays. He continues in the same letter:

> But first I would like him to pay for it as it was contracted, that is, silent, since I finished it many months ago, and it's not my responsibility if Signor Lantz hasn't submitted it yet; and Lantz has dug in his heels and doesn't want to submit it! How do you

like this! In all this business, Philips supports Eichberg, because he says Eichberg has to have the screenplay from Lantz in order to pay him; if he doesn't receive it, he can't pay for what he hasn't received. I tell him that Signor Eichberg has received my screenplay, and that I don't have to be caught in the middle, if those two are squabbling and both have dug in their heels. Philips assures me that there's no doubt that I will have my money, but I mustn't also be stubborn in claiming it, ruining everything, because, if I do so, I may lose the other two deals I already have, and in conclusion, I find myself in this nice situation; having almost run out of money, with my last 750 marks, which I have to pay to the lawyer Adler on the fifteenth in order to get back my rings and my watch, if I don't want to lose them; everything held up, my trip to London, the deals…Unbelievable stuff! All for the sake of these talking-film contraptions (p. 127).

Pirandello thus lays out the situation from which he is attempting to extricate himself, clearly finding it absurd, even comically so, were it not happening to him. As often happens to certain characters in his plays, he is manipulated by others, who in following their own interests make him feel stifled and trapped, leaving him with no escape: one thinks of the *raisonneur* figures like Mattia Pascal, Serafino Gubbio, Laudisi in *It Is So (If You Think So)*, Leone Gala in *The Rules of the Game*, Enrico IV, the Father in the *Six Characters in Search of an Author*, and Vitangelo Moscarda in *One, None and a Hundred Thousand*, among others. These figures represent the author and tend to voice the principal lessons of the plays. Moreover, it is always the world of the stage and its characters with which Pirandello feels most comfortable and which allows him to express himself most articulately. The way the author describes his present predicament, with all its seriousness, reads much like a plot outline for one of his fictional scenes.

Pirandello always maintained a contradictory stance toward film, and despite the possibilities it offered for both his artistic activity and his earnings, as well as for Marta Abba's future, on the whole it was not an unalloyed positive experience. He had forged his own path in the theater: revolutionizing techniques, provoking strong reactions among public and critics alike, and eventually emerging victorious. Sound film caught him in a moment of crisis. After the enterprise of directing the Teatro d'Arte, whose early artistic results had not reaped corresponding rewards, his playwriting career had reached a delicate pass. Disappointed by the dubious results of several recent plays such as *Diana and Tuda* and *Each His Own Way*, Pirandello was desperately looking to revamp his theatrical success as a playwright, and to renew the glory of the early 1920s, when *Six Characters in Search of an Author* had brought him international fame. It was through the film industry that he hoped to project from abroad a new artistic image of himself.

But his hope of making music-image films in Germany together with Marta Abba failed completely in the course of a few months: on March 13, 1929, the actress left again for Milan, after accompanying him to Berlin in the fall of 1928. Two days later Pirandello learned that the idea he had considered his exclusive province up to then was on the verge of being carried out by others. The very same evening, March 15, he wrote to Marta, telling her that that afternoon Lantz had visited him with a representative of the Tonfilm movie company:

> At five this gentleman arrived with Lantz. A fellow with big glasses and a face like a pickle, and a very long neck. He is a musician and an architect. His name is Doctor Tempel. Can you believe it? He has already prepared for Tonfilm four symphonies of Beethoven and two nocturnes of Chopin. My idea, already realized: my secret!
>
> You can imagine how I felt! I had been carrying my idea inside myself for almost a year! I did not want to tell it to anybody; and somebody else-this Mr. Tempel-only four months ago (as he himself confessed to me) came up with this idea and lost no time communicating it to the people at Tonfilm, who will make a mint out of it!
>
> Now the cat is out of the bag, and I don't know what I can do about it. I told Lantz and Philips that I had the idea

first; but unfortunately there is nothing I can do to stop this Mr. Tempel—who cannot be accused of stealing the idea—from using it, and rightly so. Only the consolation remains that the way I'd be able to do an interpretation of Beethoven and of Chopin he certainly will not be able to do; but in the meantime he will get the credit for the invention and for the first application of it, and this credit he will not even be able to use properly: so mediocre does he seem, and far from imagining all the ramifications that can be developed from the basic idea (Berlin, March 15, 1929; P, p. 33).

In a more hopeful vein the next day, Pirandello wrote to the actress that he had been reassured by Philips, who had told him that Mr. Lempel (and not Tempel, as Pirandello corrected himself from the previous day) was a dilettante "whom nobody takes seriously":

Yesterday Philips came back and somewhat reassured me about that gentleman from Tonfilm, whose name is Lempel and not Tempel as I wrote yesterday. The situation is not as serious as it looked at first. It seems that this Mr. Lempel is a dilettante, whom nobody takes seriously. He has attempted small mediocre projects, little experiments with poor results; and he is certainly not able to do more. He is without doubt on the same track as I am, but he does not have wings to fly. Philips has completely reassured me on this point, and now that I had to unbutton fully with him, he promised that he will put me in contact with the Americans for the full exploitation of my idea. I think he was enthusiastic about it. We'll see (Berlin, March 16, 1929; P, p. 35).

Despite the reassurances of Philips that Lempel was artistically limited, Pirandello could not sell his music-image ideas either to the German movie company Tonfilm or to the Americans whom he contacted a few months later.

Pirandello's ideas were a nearly inevitable outgrowth of the new situation in the film industry after the development of soundtracks.

Moreover, the idea that Pirandello was trying to promote as absolutely original in fact emerged from the atmosphere fostered by experimental film in the teens and twenties with which he was familiar. One thinks, for example, of the principles laid out by Marinetti in the *Manifesto of Futurist Film* (11 September 1916), when he speaks of "abstract cinema, chromatic music." This tract discussed fundamental similarities between music and film. Both, it was noted, were means of artistic expression based on rhythm. We should also keep in mind the experiments of several German avant-garde directors (Viking Eggeling, Hans Richter, Oskar Fischinger, Walter Ruttmann) who had made the first abstract films in Germany during the 1920s. Ruttmann, notably, was invited to Italy in 1934 to direct the film *Acciaio* (*Steel*), its plot taken from a story by Pirandello called *Gioca, Pietro*. This work emphasized the visual over the verbal, and incorporated methods developed a few years before in abstract films.

A common urge toward experimentation, with insights gleaned from the ever richer fount of ideas inspiring films, formed the background to what Pirandello would come to see as one of the most stinging indignities he suffered at the hands of American film. This episode concerned his contacts with Walt Disney, who, as Pirandello saw it, stole his music-image film ideas and passed them off as his own. Pirandello told Marta Abba this, and she recalled it to me many times over the course of daily conversations in the spring and summer of 1984. Marta was never specific on this charge of the Maestro's, but it was perhaps the Disney "Silly Symphonies" series, begun in 1929, that may have inspired and fuelled Pirandello's suspicions of Walt Disney. The popular series of animated shorts, in which musician Carl Stalling played a key creative role, reversed the normal emphasis on plot development backed by music, and instead adapted the animated scenes to the musical score, so that the scenes were delightful 'visualizations' of the music. Between 1929 and 1939 Disney studios made seventy-five "Silly Symphonies" shorts, including "Dancing Skeletons," "Frolicking Fish," and a series dramatizing each of the four seasons.

Although it often happens that great 'original' ideas are independently conceived of by two or more contemporary thinkers at the forefront of a scientific or artistic field, it is clear that Pirandello was already thinking, talking, and writing about the music-image film idea in 1928. Thus when series like Disney's "Silly Symphonies" began to appear in 1929, Pirandello's sense of his creative idea having been usurped and even stolen from him is understandable (if not necessarily a matter of fact). The idea of using music in a new way to generate and drive visual presentation was clearly coming into prominence on several fronts in the United States, in Britain, and Germany—Tonfilm, Disney, etc.—beginning in 1929. It is clear from Pirandello's letters that he was certainly in the creative vanguard on this idea. More importantly, however, he *felt* that he was in that vanguard—indeed, at the very forefront. He was in direct contact with producers and businessmen concerning his idea. He entrusted them with it. And though there is no evidence for this, it is certainly not implausible that these figures, in seeking to develop Pirandello's idea (for him or not), may well have been the agents of its dissemination into the wider film world.

But whatever the case, it is clear that from 1928 on Pirandello took a double-pronged interest in film: on the one hand, he was fascinated by film understood as music and images alone, and therefore clearly distinguished from the theater; on the other hand, if dialogue instead of music had to be used, Pirandello desired a cinematic transposition of his own works. But market forces were constraining him to abandon the idea of the music-image in favor of words and images. Before they moved to Germany together, he wrote from Rome to Marta Abba in this vein:

> I am only thinking right now about settings to design for films. I've already come up with seven. Each is laid out, almost scene for scene, and divided into sections of four and five parts. Even *L'Esclusa* (*The Outcast*), you can be sure. [Pirandello, in a previous letter, had mentioned that his novel *L'Esclusa* would be one of the films that he would like to make in Germany.] Everything is very interesting, full of movement, clever tricks, and of intense drama. All that has to happen is for them to succeed spectacularly, and our fortune is made (Rome, September 26, 1928; L, p. 57).

As we can see, Marta Abba is an essential part of Pirandello's cinematographic dreams. Through these the author was nourishing hopes of repeating in film the success he had obtained with Marta in the first period of the Teatro d'Arte. But the Maestro was unable to forge a movie career for Marta in Berlin. So after she returned to Milan to resume her career on stage, Pirandello decided to help her by providing new works for the company she was forming.

For most of 1929 Pirandello, finding himself still in Germany in the midst of feverish artistic activity both in film and theater, worked on the play *Come tu mi vuoi* (*As You Desire Me*) for Marta, a play in which the cinematic influence of G.W. Pabst's *Pandora's Vase* (or *Lulu*) is clear. Besides the film's decadent atmosphere, which seems to pervade the entire first act of the play, Pirandello, in delineating the character of the Unknown and her many ambiguities, must have had in mind the ambiguities rendered by the actress Louise Brooks with her subtle, silent expressive art. Not to mention that the obsessive passion of Salter and his daughter Mop for the Unknown is a duplication of what is felt for the film's protagonist first by her widower (who, like Salter, also uses a pistol) and then by her girlfriend.

Two Characters in Search of a Filmmaker

But if, for Marta, the transition from the stage to the movie camera was difficult at this point, for Pirandello it was even more full of snares. The most striking example was undoubtedly the tortuous path that led to the making of the film version of the *Six Characters*. This work, which had made Pirandello internationally famous, nevertheless met with impossible obstacles in the attempts to turn it into a film. Between 1928 and 1936, Pirandello wrote to his son Stefano and to friends, collaborators, agents and directors, making constant reference to the many attempts to realize the project. In letters to Marta, he confides his hopes of seeing this work, written several years before, brought to life on screen—a hope upon which he sometimes seems to believe that his very life depends. Similarly, *The Mountain Giants*, a play born from a profound crisis, written with the author's relationship with Marta in mind, exhibits traits of the very contingencies which accompanied its coming into being. Both projects envision the philosophical perfection with which Pirandello desired to conclude his artistic career. In his last drama as well as the potential film version of the *Six Characters*, Pirandello places not only all the creative energy he has left, but also his entire artistic and literary experience, which expresses his irresolution and the contradictions tearing him apart, producing a sort of prophetic allegory.

In fact, the screenplay is hardly a mere adaptation of the play to the different medium of film. It constitutes, rather, a complete transformation of the text of the original. It is a delirious, quasi-hallucinatory intensification of the mechanisms of division and mirror reflection, which, rather than multiplying figures and situations, ends up concentrating them into just two characters, the father and the stepdaughter. The six characters of the title are thus reduced to two, while the actors, director, stage hands, and so forth are all eliminated. Even the author for whom they were searching is now present as if he had been found, since among the various mirror images of the father there is one of Pirandello himself, who is the author not only of the characters that have been dancing around in his head, but also of himself. Moreover, the countless Pirandellian characters are merely the result—fantastic and creative—of the division and the reflection in infinite fragments of a self compelled to multiply itself in order to create the illusion of its existence, like a broken mirror, which infinitely reflects an integrity that could not exist in and of itself.

By examining the transformation that the screenplay underwent, we realize why the least autobiographical of Italian writers can also be regarded as the most autobiographical. The characters never represent the 'other' but rather the infinite, and infinitely deformed, phenomenology of the self. It is for good reason that Pirandello, who was so private and so removed from the slightest hint of conspicuousness, made the surprising condition that the film version should make him the leading man, playing opposite the leading lady, the Stepdaughter/Marta Abba. Now, this condition is not what it may seem to be—a mere sentimental weakness, or a pathetic attempt to attach the actress more closely to himself in an almost 'public' bond. It is, rather, a process of reducing to their core the defense mechanisms through which the author-character-actor circuit is viewed, in its hidden recesses, as if it were an object rendered totally transparent. 'Autobiographical,' therefore, is used in the following sense: in the moment of his intense love for the young actress, Pirandello reveals his intimate weaknesses, such as his inability to face the 'other' because it is the other, and the deep distress caused by the loss of self in the 'blindness' of love.

The six screen characters, just like those in the stage play, are therefore performers in a mythical tale in which incest is a symbol of the impossibility of love—except that in the screenplay the psychological games are more open, because the one who is in the position of loving, or of wanting to seduce, the Stepdaughter/Marta Abba, is the Father/Pirandello. The aged author fully experiences once again the shame for the erotic attraction that the elderly protagonist (of the fragment of a novel on which the play *Six Characters* is based) felt when he was going up the stairs of a brothel where he was to meet a young student: incest is a superimposition that brings to the stage, in the classical Oedipal figure, the guilty shame of sexuality.

Pirandello makes himself a character among his characters in order to explain that his choice is entirely literary, at the same moment that real love ignites all his anguish and sets in motion his defense mechanisms. From one perspective the screenplay's curious casting plan is a devious—and ingenious—last-ditch effort by Pirandello to realize his fantasies for real intimacy through the staged façade of a movie screen. But from another perspective it is *still unreal*—the barrier of dramatic representation and staging is still not broken. Even though Pirandello and Marta would be playing the parts, it would still be a performance, an act. Pirandello has only succeeded in uniting himself, his 'real' self, all the more closely with the fictions of his fantasy manifested in his scripts.

The Hand that Turns the Crank

The impressions made by film in the cultural environment of those early years must have been especially vivid, especially compared to the written word. In *Six Characters*, Pirandello demonstrates the difficulties of words: how awkward they can be, how deficient as bearers of communication. Pirandello puts apposite words in the mouth of the Father:

> "But can't you see that all the trouble lies here! In the words! All of us have a world full of things! And how can we understand one another, sir, if in the words I speak I put the meaning and the value of things as I myself see them, while the one who listens inevitably takes them according to the meaning and the value which he has in himself of the world he has inside of *himself*. We think we understand each other, we never understand one another."

Pirandello is thinking of the multivalent meanings of words and the many possible resonances words can evoke in listeners, both through their surface meanings and by way of analogy. What defines and presents the meaning of a word is the structure of the context, the syntax, word order, and the sense of the narrative as a whole. But to understand the thread is not merely to understand what is expressly said, but also what is left unsaid, and what *cannot* be said. On the contrary, movie images have the great advantage, and at the same time the serious limitation, of being an absolutely clear manifestation: all things can be shown, but nothing else. The emotions they arouse are psychological effects in the most deterministic sense of the phrase. To say that emotions elicited by a word are 'an effect' is not exactly right, for the meaning of a word is not limited by the immediate effect it creates, but rather extends itself and is enriched through successive layers of interpretation.

Pirandello therefore probably felt that this new genre provided unlimited liberty to reveal himself more intimately. All conventional expectations are laid aside in the situations represented through human characters, gestures, and expressions on the screen. We should keep in mind that the very darkness of the movie theater cuts the spectators off from one another, allowing each to take part individually and privately in the events affecting the characters. There is an escape from the hold of everyday categories as the emotions are given free play. The spectator's eyes are fascinated, taken aback by the spectacle, and entranced by the human faces that elicit the greatest possible reaction from the crowd. The distance between audience and characters that was imposed by screen technology led to an almost magical concentration on the faces of characters. We know, in fact, that Pirandello was spellbound by the movies and enjoyed their spectacle regularly. Marta's sister Cele Abba proudly recalled to me in the spring of 1984 how she would accompany Pirandello on his many trips to the cinema, while Marta was devoting herself to intensive study and rehearsal at home.

At the same time, Pirandello seemed to be freer to express feelings and emotions that life suggested, and which he could express in an artistic form more easily through the safety of the projected and detached motion picture. To get some idea of the almost existential significance Pirandello attributed to the film version of the *Six Characters,* we can consider in detail some references he made to the subject at various times in letters to Marta Abba. Toward the beginning of his plans for the film, in July 1928, he wrote:

> Please do not think that I have neglected to give long, steady, and increasingly productive thoughts to the scenario of *Six Characters*. I have it by now almost all completed in my mind. As soon as we're together, in Genoa, I'll explain it to you for your approval and, who knows, maybe also your collaboration, because I want this work to be in everything and for everything OURS, born from THE TWO OF US, one thing only and OURS. You'll see how many ideas I have thought about, and how well it will come out; and everything will be clear, extraordinarily powerful on the levels of fantasy and drama!" (Nettuno, July 13, 1928; P, pp. 21-22)

Several months later the project seemed on the verge of taking off:

> The other piece of news is from Bernstiel, who tells me he's just returned to Milan from a trip abroad and shows signs of being quite dismayed by all the talk in Germany about the film of the *Six Characters* for which I will be cast. He says the company with which he is cutting the deal for the three films is concerned about the film of the *Six Characters*, which should earn worldwide film interest and cast every other deal into the shade. I answered him reassuringly, saying that right now nothing definite has been done about the *Six Characters* and if the company he's dealing with is so concerned and interested in this film, we would like nothing better than to write a contract with them for the *Six Characters* also, provided that that arrangement will not interfere with the deals for the other three films. I wrote to him also, saying he should be ready to leave with us at the beginning of October, and that I shall be in Milan on the 28th to discuss everything" (Rome, September 23, 1928; L, p. 52).

Despite these promising beginnings, however, after five months in Berlin Pirandello was still far from settling a firm deal. On March 16, 1929, he wrote to Marta, who had just returned from Milan:

> Negotiations are still going on for the *Six Characters*, and Philips has the greatest confidence that we'll be able to conclude the deal soon (P, p. 35).

A week later, returning to the same subject, he wrote to Marta:

> Philips is waiting for the arrival of Mr. Blumenthal from the United States, a director or one of the big shots from Paramount. He claims to be interested in the *Six Characters*; he should be in Berlin in a few days, because he is already on his way and Philips will bring him to me so I can talk to him about the idea of musical films. He is still showing himself very optimistic and he's suggesting that I be patient, since big

deals are definitely in the works (Berlin, March 21, 1929; L, p. 79).

And again, a few days later:

> As far as Tonfilm, I think, beyond the American interests, whom I'm going to meet with on April 3rd, there are very eager parties from London; and one's coming today at five to talk to me. He had asked me anxiously by telegram whether I didn't have other projects I had done before now. And the making of the *Six Characters* will probably also be with Tonfilm, either in the United States or in London (Berlin, March 26, 1929; L, pp. 92-93).

By this point Pirandello was beginning to realize that making a film of *Six Characters* would not be as easy as he had expected. The film industry was in turmoil, and it seemed that his carefully laid plans would come to naught. On this score he wrote to Marta a month later:

> Well yes, I also believe we are far from signing the deal for the *Six Characters*, even though Philips was saying up until a few nights ago he wouldn't give up a deal that certainly would be made, even if they would give him not just 2000, but 5000 marks. But at the moment, the whole film world is upside down as a result of these talking films, which are making such a noise everywhere that no one speaks of anything else. It is likely that one hears such talk in Italy as well, if what Stefano has told me recently is to be believed, about the intentions of Bisi towards me. In that case what You are saying in Your letter will happen; I would be connected with a large concern, which needs a head, in order not to be running on empty. We shall see (Berlin, April 11, 1929, L, pp. 124-5).

Unfortunately, news arriving from Italy brought no solid business footings either. We can infer this from a letter written to Marta Abba in which he quotes a letter he had just received from his son Stefano:

> As far as film business goes, Stefano writes to me that Interlandi has already spoken three times with Antongini, Bisi's secretary, and twice with Bisi himself, everyone says they're in the best and most favorable mood towards you and ready to make your films, even the *Six Characters*; but for now one cannot do more than talk about them, because the production cannot begin for another ten months, which are needed before the first sets of the firm which is to build an honest-to-goodness *Citta del cinematografo* [City of cinematography] can be up and running. Bisi tells me he will write to you soon (Berlin, March 19, 1929; L, p. 75).

The references to the desire to make *Six Characters*, which were equaled by the hopes of making new contacts that would allow him to make new films soon, therefore became a recurrent theme not only of the letters sent to Marta until a few days before his death, but also of those written to his son Stefano, who was looking after his father's interests in Rome, and to the stage director Guido Salvini, for whom Pirandello admitted having the deepest respect and an unconditional trust.

Aside from the fact that Pirandello had his own distinctive vision of the film industry, he continued to nourish until the very end the hope that it could become a new source of success and wealth, both for Marta Abba and for him. Concerned about her future in Italy, the actress had written to him from Milan after leaving Berlin in disappointment. Pirandello responded that he was willing to help her financially, and to organize a new company:

> After paying in April the rest of my debts to the Banca Commerciale, I'll get from Toplitz in September a new line of credit to be used as the financial base for the new company. I know Toplitz, I know his wife, I know Mattioli, the personal secretary of Toplitz; I have every possible connection with the Banca Commerciale. A line of credit of at least 150 thousand

lire will be open for me, unless in the meantime (that is, between now and September) I happen to make the big money I expect from the movies, in which case there would be no need of anything (Berlin, March 28, 1929; P, p. 49).

Eager at the prospects, Pirandello wrote another letter two days later in the same optimistic vein:

> I am going to London with Eichberg to sign a contract for two more films, before leaving, tomorrow or the day after tomorrow, I'll meet with the Americans here. I've already prepared my memo, in which I explain my new idea, with the greatest clarity and efficacy; if the idea is accepted, Marta, our fortune is made; we'll do whatever we want to do (Berlin, April 1, 1929; P, p. 57).

Between optimistic highs and devastating setbacks, Pirandello would leave nothing untried in nearly eight years of effort to make a film version of the *Six Characters*, first in Berlin, and then in London, Rome, Paris and Hollywood. Here at last he still hoped, just a few days before his death, that the film would be directed by Max Reinhardt (with whom he had quarreled about several of his directorial efforts on the stage). Reinhardt, as we mentioned earlier, had in the meantime moved to the United States because of the outbreak of Nazi racial persecutions in Germany. Pirandello poured the story of these eight years into the letters he sent not only to Marta but also to his children, friends, agents, and in those vague and often-repeated phrases which become the vessel of a higher hope transcending the mere making of the *Six Characters* and expressing his desire for success and gain, both for himself and for Marta Abba.

But film and America itself, as the components of a single, impossible dream, remained deaf to the writer's last, dramatic cry. And he, disappointed and now thoroughly disabused of any serious interest in the art form, unleashed his hostility in letters to Marta shortly before his death. He affixed to these words the epilogue to his experience with film:

> These dealings are good for nothing except to exhaust and disgust you, especially to disgust you. Disgust is the strongest impression that you get from American life [...]
> (New York, August 13, 1935; L, p. 1215).

> [American filmmakers] do despise what they say they are forced to do, and therefore you cannot argue with them [...] I'm thoroughly disgusted! (New York, August 30, 1935; P, p. 296).

> All the movies I see are stupid and crude, and [filmmakers] are more stubborn than ever in persisting in this stupidity and crudeness, firm in their belief that the audience doesn't want anything else. There's no way out (New York, September 7, 1935; L, p. 1221).

In the Artist's Studio

Luigi Pirandello's fascination with moviemaking was only one side of his deep and lifelong artistic engagement with the visual arts. His intense fixation in the twenties and thirties on achieving success in the modern world of moving pictures did not prevent him from nurturing his love for the more traditional visual media of painting. Throughout his life he practiced landscape painting, which was how he spent the last summer of his life while staying with his son Fausto, himself a professional painter. In the course of my conversations with her, Marta often referred to this aspect of Pirandello's creative activities: "[the Maestro] painted little paintings, trees, coastlines; he was a great landscape painter. And he was most dexterous at painting. One summer, at Viareggio, I was posing for a portrait by Primo Conti. Pirandello put in his own suggestions...nuances."

Several exhibits of Pirandello's paintings have been held over the years.

The first was held in 1938 at Trajan's Market in Rome, shortly after Pirandello's death, and two prominent events were put on in the 1980s in Italy. These exhibits have made the writer's oil and pastel paintings available for public viewing. His diverse subjects included landscapes of Anticoli, the house of his son Fausto, landscapes of the Tuscan countryside (San Marcello Pistoiese), the beach of the pine groves of Viareggio, many family portraits (of his sons Stefano and Fausto, and of his grandchildren), the unforgettable country surrounding Caos, the Sicilian estate where the writer was born, and the nearby coast of Porto Empedocle.

Pirandello's style, technique, and subjects show a loyalty to antiquated notions of quaint domesticated images in an artistic medium that was certainly more than just a mere hobby. Looking at these paintings one can feel their creator's desire to express himself, as well as a sense that he was seeking out shapes that would allow him to paint according to the old, tested rules. Even if Pirandello's taste in painting has been considered conventional, even retrograde, we can nevertheless discern a certain evolution of choices that allowed him to approach, through various phases, both the best in conventional nineteenth-century Italian tastes and, secondly, the poetic and deeply idiosyncratic style of the so-called "Roman school" of the 1920s. On the one hand, he cautiously accepted novelties, and on the other he showed a certain resistance and disdain toward those forms or ways that seem to depart from traditional canons.

Pirandello's theater was revolutionary and provocative. His plays tended to disorient, shaking the very foundations of traditional theater and provoking intensely polemical reactions. At first sight, little remains of this apocalyptic vision in his paintings. Especially in his earliest paintings, the revolutionary playwright seemed to conform to the most conventional canons of the painterly tradition, which is still linked to a kind of late nineteenth-century realism. What sense could it have made for a man in the process of revolutionizing theater to paint in strict accordance with artistic canons that seemed long outdated? But perhaps there exists a deeper affinity between his literary activities and his painting that belies appearances. It is true that in his painting he was not proclaiming a revolution in content and form, as he was in his dramatic productions. And yet behind the apparent calm of his visual works, in the heterogeneous plans of realization and the variety of compositions, there are clear signs of inner struggle and urgent questions. The prominent art critic Emilio Cecchi (1884-1966) wrote in the catalogue of the first show in 1938 devoted to Pirandello's paintings:

> He comes to think that this modest and careful painting served him above all as a kind of meditation [...] Seated before Reality, he analyzed it with his brush, in order not to later unconsciously mix in his writing the two processes, of painting and of literature. Perhaps it consisted mainly of a means of literary integrity.
>
> By this means, indeed, the evolution of his taste and his knowledge, and his garnering of a more free and expressive touch of modernity, are very clear. The oldest among these impressions, reflect his low-key and unspectacular nineteenth-century realism. While in the more recent ones the rendering of reality is more sour and at the same time more ethereal, the brushwork more suggestive, all within the boundaries and tones of a dry, scorched and by no means sensual sensibility, which is at the heart of the entire Pirandellian mood ("Luigi Pirandello pittore," p. 92).

Cecchi certainly seems to have hit the mark in saying that painting for Pirandello was "a form of meditation." Indeed, for Pirandello painting was an ideal workshop for analysis, where he expressed, through the intensity of colors, the trials and tribulations of the painter-protagonists we find in his short stories and plays. However, painting was not simply an activity of study and practice. Every work that Pirandello set to accomplish demanded total involvement, and constituted a strict trial in life. But the use he made of painting was to achieve the sort of freedom that comes by escaping one's usual routine; it allowed him to express all that remained as constraints on him while he was occupied with his principal artistic activity—in other words, life without the mask of the theater. If the mask hides life, discarding it leads to a substantially different reality: that which is born out of painting with freedom and autonomy, but always according to tried and true rules, and therefore remote from the problematic complexity experienced by Pirandello's characters in the theater, and closer, if anything, to a calmness which he longed for throughout his turbulent existence. There is also the possibility that, with his conventional manner of painting, Pirandello was insulating and distancing himself from the official art of the regime,—the kind of painting, architecture, and sculpture promoted by Mussolini that prevailed, often with catastrophic results of bad taste.

There is a letter written to Marta Abba in which Pirandello, gazing out on the groves of Nettuno, a beachside town near Rome, in the deep silence of the summer night, confesses that he wished he had his box of paints to paint two huge cypresses that loomed out of the depths of the pine grove. His description of the sight that he wanted to paint for the actress contained all the visual intensity and chromatic richness of a painting:

> I'd love to have my paints here with me. Looking at the pine grove I am overcome with an immense longing to paint. I wish I could make you at least a sketch of this scene. The gray skeletons of two huge cypresses loom over the other dark green, sun-drenched trees. One is a little bent, very sad-looking; the other, on the contrary, is straight and powerful. It gives me great pain to look at it among so many living fellow trees; all dried up and without a single leaf, but still completely whole in the texture of the twigs and branches that outlined its crown on the once vigorous trunk. I am sure that if I had brushes, palette and colors I could well express this pain (Nettuno [Rome], July 5, 1928; P, p. 17).

As often happens in Pirandello's theatrical situations, even this image, which at first sight could pass for a traditional and perhaps predictable oil painting, takes on an increasingly dramatic meaning. Indeed, right after describing the landscape that he would like to depict, Pirandello suggests to Marta: "[…] and you, some time later, looking at this tree, dead but still standing among the ones that are smaller but still alive, you would think…" (p. 17).

At this point, as we see, the thought is interrupted by an ellipsis, which we are left to interpret, but which suggests many possible readings. There is of course the writer's hope the actress will remember him after his death. Then there is a large question mark—what will Marta think? And this raises the somber melancholy of the fact that the question gazes forward to the time when the Maestro will have passed away. The long description then turns to more lyrical tones, and the landscape fills with cicadas:

> But away with gloomy thoughts! If you could only hear this shrill, insistent chirping of the cicadas! Maybe, by this time, they have started to chirp in the trees of the park in front of your hotel. It's a dear voice of the summer, though, this chirping of the cicadas (p. 17).

In order that Marta, while vacationing in Salsomaggiore, might also listen to that "dear voice of the summer," the painting Pirandello describes then becomes more sharply defined and is enriched with the memory of the night before, when the moon was shining with its reflection on the water, dominating all things:

> Last night I sat out on the terrace until two A.M., just watching the moon on the sea. And I was thinking that it is a standing joke to say that nowadays people do not care about the moon anymore, since every city street has plenty of moons in rows. Yes, many; but one street lamp lights a twenty-yard circle; with this moon, on the other hand, while I was watching it this night on the sea, Marta could see it from her window over the trees of the park in Salsomaggiore. And I could picture you at the window of your little room….But

you, certainly, at two A.M. of this night, must have been asleep in your bed (p. 17).

Marta never received either the sketch with the dead tree from the Nettuno pine grove or any other of the paintings that he made with great enthusiasm at various other times in his life. In her Milan residence, the actress had two portraits of Pirandello, one of them painted by the well-known painter Primo Conti. During one of our conversations she confessed to me that she lacked even a single painting from Pirandello's hand. "I regret," she said,

> that I do not have a single painting by the Maestro: I have so many things of his, books, annotated scripts of plays, letters, photographs, but I don't have even a single painting of his. More than once the Maestro wanted to give me one, but, for whatever reason, I always procrastinated. I always used to say 'Later, later'. The Maestro painted a lot in the summer of '36, while I was in London rehearsing and practicing before going with the play to Broadway, and he was at Anticoli, the village of Fausto's wife, whom he was visiting at the time.

It is likely that, if Pirandello had painted for the actress the painting as described in the letter, his pictorial language would have fit perfectly with that expressed in all his other paintings. Yet the themes that come out of the description of the scene are not far removed from those we are used to see emerging from the fabric of his literary works: the 'straight' and nearly skeletal cypress opposed to the other green and flourishing trees, the presence of death and of the moon, and the multiple meanings that it has in relation to the internal wounds symbolized by the trees. It is possible that painting can better accommodate that energetic idyllic quality which the moon seems to represent, but in strict correspondence with the phenomenology of existential anguish. In this sense, the idyllic by its very nature is indescribable, and is therefore better rendered with the allusive rather than explicit art of painting.

The Hand that Turns the Crank

At the beginning of the same picturesque letter, Pirandello writes that he has found lodging in the Albergo Nettunia, and describes the view from his window:

> I am writing from Nettuno, where I found a beautiful room here in the Albergo Neptunia, with a window overlooking the magnificent villa of the Borghese princes—the one surrounded by the famous pine grove. A wide terrace faces the sea, with Porto d'Anzio on the right, and the ancient Castello d'Astura far away to the left on the horizon. Everything is peaceful here. The silence in the pine grove is eroded by the steady chirping of the cicadas and embroidered with the merry sound of the birds. And over there, the wideness of the sea sparkles in the sunshine (pp. 16-7).

In this passage Pirandello again describes another precise and well-structured sketch of a possible painting. And even though in his vast literary production there are few visual indulgences, in the letters to Marta Abba he will occasionally linger over expansive descriptions of idyllic settings and landscapes, particularly in moments of great lyricism. These tend to adhere to the rules of a well-known rhetorical tradition in describing or suggesting the writer's love, delusions, jealousy, loneliness, doubts, hopes, and anxiety. For example, in the loneliness of Berlin where Marta had left him, Pirandello's state of mind seems to find a congenial analogue in the still wintry cityscape of April 1929, which was decidedly lacking in the comforts of spring: "[…] all the houses' roofs, and the trees, and the streets, are white with snow, as in the heart of winter, and last night […] when I returned at 9:30 from Aida [a restaurant], I seemed like a snow statue, utterly frozen" (Berlin, April 7, 1929; L, p. 118).

Painting was no doubt a constant presence in Pirandello's life. Besides his own work in this field, there was also that of his son Fausto, a noted painter who died in 1975 and whose work Pirandello always followed with a careful and anxious eye. Because of the constant attention and worry he devoted to the artistic activities of Fausto, who was far from a conventional painter and who was influenced not only by the new styles he saw in Italy but also those he saw abroad and especially in Paris, Pirandello maintained a connection with controversies over painting and art in general. There was also his activity both as an art critic and as a painter, all of which provided him with many diverse experiences that led him to ponder both the theoretical and technical aspects of art, and that no doubt influenced his views on aesthetics generally.

At times Pirandello offered his son fatherly artistic advice, for example in a letter written in July, 1928 to Fausto, who was then in Paris seeking out his own style of expression:

> You need to free yourself from your whole concern with 'modernity' and stop painting just the same way everyone paints, namely, hideously [...] In Venice I saw works of modern artists: unspeakable things on one side, and inane academism on the other. [...] If you are determined to think in your own special way, which you are capable of expressing in such a precise way in your letters, well then, paint these thoughts of yours. You will be true to yourself, and will express yourself: you will express something substantial (Venturi, *Pirandello oltre la maschera*).

This is one example of the often described relationship between the literary father and his painter son, and shows very clearly the cultural split between Luigi and Fausto Pirandello. Fausto's actual artistic choices seem almost never to have been in line with his father's suggestions. Nonetheless, we can surmise that the paternal critique and rejection expressed here may well have produced a reciprocal relationship of artistic constraint and engagement between father and son.

But in contrast with the understanding we can glean of the relations between Pirandello and his son from the correspondence between the two, which is always rich, observant, and full of news and hopes, the letters written to Marta Abba provide a fuller understanding of the situation. In writing to Marta, Pirandello on several occasions refers to his son's artistic

The Hand that Turns the Crank

activity, in some cases expressing, along with his usual cares, opinions which are swayed by paternal affection. Writing from Rome in September, 1928, to Marta, who was then in Milan, Pirandello tells her that Ferreira, a French film agent involved in plans to film the *Six Characters*, had written him from Paris, giving him news of his son Fausto, who "is very well and working for an exposition." Several months later (March 1929), Pirandello wrote from Berlin to Marta, who had just returned to Milan:

> My dear Marta, yesterday I ended up going to Solari's. I arrived (it was the fault of your dear little alarm clock) a quarter of an hour late. There I found Aponte of the *Corriere*, Boiano of the *Popolo d'Italia* [Italian newspaper correspondents in Berlin], and Ivo Pannaggi [an Italian painter living in Berlin] who was admiring some of Fausto's daubs, which Solari was showing around" (Berlin, March 15, 1929; P, p. 32).

And again the next day:

> ...speaking of Paris, this morning I received one of the usual letters from Fausto, full of bitterness. It looks as if Vildrac did not organize things as he should have. He sold a few paintings and some drawings. But very few visitors came to see the show. He hopes he will have more today (Saturday) and tomorrow (Sunday) (Berlin, March 16, 1929; P, p. 36).

Just as often as in his letters, Pirandello's references to Fausto's painting would crop up in his conversations with Marta Abba. During one of our meetings she recalled: "The beginnings, as often happens, were not easy for Fausto. I remember that when he had exhibits the Maestro sent someone to buy incognito one of his son's works, to cheer him up. I had a painting by Fausto, but then I sold it to a gallery owner who was collecting his paintings. I didn't know what to do with a single painting." Abba's sister Cele added her memory of an experience with Fausto: "I was fond of Fausto, but I never understood the way he painted. On one occasion he asked me if he could paint my portrait, and I agreed. But when I saw the bright red nose he had given me, I stood straight up and walked out."

So intimate was the friendship that bound him to the actress for the last ten years of his life that Pirandello never hesitated to convey to Marta all the anxieties that assailed him, even those relating to his family. The actress remained involved in situations that might seem marginal, both to the world of the theater and to her relations with the man who wrote specifically for her, from 1925 on, the majority of his theatrical works. Marta in fact seemed to have a prominent place in the artist's visual imagination, becoming the most fleshed-out figure of the entire correspondence. It naturally consists of moments that conjure her up, along with the surroundings in which she moved, through words. And even if Pirandello never painted her on canvas, certain of Marta's 'moments,' described over the course of his letters to her, probably helped to delineate many scenes for the same female characters whom Marta would later interpret on stage with perfect fidelity.

Two descriptions, both in letters written from Rome in August, 1926, are characteristic of these moments. Tersely, but with great nuance, Pirandello gives life to two paintings or, if you prefer, two sketches to be performed. In the first one, having received from Marta a "fresh morning letter," he writes:

> I breathe the 'still biting air of the night' entering from the little balcony of your dining room—with so much open space in front of it. And I see you as you look in the morning, a bit chilly as you write to me (Rome, August 17, 1926; P, p. 8).

Several days later Pirandello writes to the actress about *Their Wives' Girlfriend*, saying that he can't wait for her to read the script so that he might see on her face her impression upon reading it: "I enjoyed it so much while you were reading *Diana and Tuda* in Livorno, do you remember? In the vast well-lit room, with that balcony opening onto a view of the sea..." (Rome, August 24, 1926; L, p. 23).

In both these descriptions a figure of a woman stands in front of, or at least close to, a balcony opening onto a landscape that serves as a backdrop for the figure herself. In these two scenes Pirandello records the actress at a precise moment when the balcony is "open to a view of the sea"—following a technical device reminiscent of Matisse in that happy phase of his art when the rich and mixed gallery of women he depicted in front of an open balcony on the shore at Nice came to life. The series of female figures who posed for Matisse in front of a balcony, whether open or closed, began around 1918, after the painter moved to the Cote d'Azur in 1916. From those years we have *Le thé du matin* (1920), *Interieur a Nice, Femme assise avec un livre* (1920), *Interieur a Nice, la sieste* (1922); *Femme assise, le dos tourne vers la fenetre ouverte* (1921-1923), to mention just a few in which sensual female figures are depicted languorously posed before the balcony, or occasionally before a window. Pirandello seems to appeal to the same pictorial motifs when he describes Marta on the balcony, in the colorful tones which his pictorial sense allows him to offer, in an intertextual game between word and graphic sign, albeit lacking sensuality and with a dominant place allotted to romanticized nature.

But even more relevant here is a poem that Pirandello had written long before in his youth, entitled "Primavera dei Terrazzi" ("Springtime on the Terraces"). In it he describes a woman coming out onto her terrace:

> The neighbor woman, on an April morning
> Still embraced by the warmth of her bed
> Comes out on the terrace, and to the sun of spring
> Offers the treasure of her abundant breast....
> So, among the flowers, on the balustrade
> Among the vases well-ordered and with love
> Cultivated by her throughout the year
> She seems herself to be a living flower...
> (in *Saggi, poesie, scritti varii*).

He had penned this poem's lovely visual scene decades before he ever met Marta Abba—indeed, before he had even turned his literary talents to writing plays. Obviously long-possessed by this almost archetypal image of a woman on her balcony, Pirandello's descriptions of times when Marta does the same are even more evocative, and suffused with untold emotion and associations for the author, summoning up, not least, the now long past springtime idylls of his youth.

Chapter 4

A STAR IS (NOT QUITE) BORN

When I met with Marta Abba in Milan in the spring of 1984 to go through the hundreds of old letters she had written to and received from the Maestro, nearly fifty years had passed since his death. In her mid-thirties when he died, Marta was now over eighty, and though still a striking woman with a remarkable personality and penetrating green eyes, the years had worn on her. After all, it had not been an easy half century for her. In the wake of the death of Pirandello, who had played an essential if not always effective role in her life, Marta was alone with her success for the first time. She no longer had Luigi's constant paternal, almost nagging voice in her ear, or his protection and concern with creating opportunities for them—always together—in theater, and more recently in film. Nor had he in his final years quite achieved the definitive and resounding success in film that he had hoped for. Had he done so, Marta's career might have been on a better footing in a world that was increasingly turned toward film as the preferred medium for acting stardom.

When he died in December, 1936, however, Marta was far from having made the successful shift to film acting that might well have given her career the momentum it needed to sustain itself in the void created by his absence. As it stood, his absence remained an active force in her life, as the traces of the lives of those we have been close to invariably do, though the after-effects of her relationship with Pirandello were not always pleasant or benign. In the fifty years that had passed between then and my visits with her, she had learned to adjust to life in a strange and foreign country, the Midwestern United States, in a marriage of convenience that ended twelve years later in a messy divorce. When Marta returned to Italy in the 1950s after her divorce, she faced further troubles, legal, personal, and career-related, all of them in one way or another connected with the brief, bright life she had had with her former Maestro. Nevertheless, she overcame her various adversities and had emerged with a significant fortune from her divorce settlement, as well as the rights to nine of Pirandello's plays. But the years of fighting, defending, and maintaining her image as the glorious actress—the 'Pirandellian' actress—had left her somewhat bitter, and now, at her age, slightly paranoid.

But one thing she had never quite attained was a real lasting love, which might have sweetened her days of petty irritations and frustrations—an intimate other with whom she could share her soul and the warmth of touch. She had experienced something of love with the Maestro, chaste though it was; she did not, it would seem, with her American husband; and so, for other reasons too, which we will come to later, for her Venus would remain an elusive goddess.

It was a unique and moving experience to hold in my hands and read, with Marta there reminiscing about and elaborating on the events referred to, old letters that attested to a bygone age in Marta's life, one full of vigor and promise, of energy and activity, of the fond hopes and vain ambitions of a great artist whose mind was still strong but whose body was slowly failing. From the letters, from what Marta told me as we spoke together, and from later research, there emerge details of her twilight days with the Maestro and her long life after his passing that make up the final chapters of the story.

Despite the inevitable difficulties of the theater business, matters went fairly well for Marta while the Maestro was still alive: the actress, thanks to her indisputable talent, succeeded in making herself known in Italy and abroad, performing both in Italian and in French. The Paris version of *Man, Beast and Virtue* had been a hit, and made waves in its English version as well, both in London and America. But it was in vain that Pirandello tried to introduce the actress into the world of film, particularly when the screenplay was drawn from his own works; in this new medium of entertainment Marta never really made her mark.

The episode that may have brought about the most crushing disillusionment, the bitter details of which the octogenarian actress still remembered, concerned the making of the film *Acciaio*, a screenplay Pirandello wrote with his son Stefano in 1933 (they had adapted it from one of his short stories, *Gioca, Pietro!*, and the screenplay originally bore the same title). The leading female role had been promised to Marta Abba but was given at the last minute to a younger actress, Isa Pola. As Marta recounted to me in the spring of 1984, the person responsible for the last-minute substitution, in addition to the German director Walter Ruttmann, was Emilio Cecchi, who was at that time artistic director of Cines, a newly founded film studio company. Ruttmann was at that time a big name in the field of documentary-experimental film, but differed widely in sensibility from the Sicilian writer. For his part Pirandello, disappointed both by the exclusion of Marta and by the work Ruttmann had done—his work had completely misunderstood the Pirandellian mood of the screenplay—demanded from the studio that in the opening credits it should be spelled out that the film was "loosely based on a story by Luigi Pirandello."

Marta Abba had only the briefest of movie acting careers. She played leading roles in two films, *Il caso Haller* (1933) directed by Alessandro Blasetti, and *Teresa Confalonieri* (1934), directed by Guido Brignone. The latter film, about an aristocratic woman who played an important role in the nineteenth-century Italian Risorgimento, won the Golden Lion prize at the Venice Film Festival. On that occasion Marta recalled meeting Katherine Hepburn, who was introduced at the Festival as the "new star." She wrote about this to Pirandello on August 8, 1934, from the Excelsior Palace Hotel in Venice: "the movies I have seen so far at the festival have not made much of an impression on me. It is true that the American Colossuses will begin to be shown tonight, with the presentation of the new star Katherine Hepburn" (C, p. 264). Hepburn received the prize of Best Actress that year for her performance in *Little Women* (1933); the previous year she had won her first Academy Award for her third film appearance in *Morning Glory* (1933).

Teresa Confalonieri was released in the U.S. in 1937 under the title *Loyalty of Love*. At the time Marta was performing in *Tovarich* on Broadway. The film was poorly reviewed in the *New York Times*, though her performance was described as its sole redeeming consolation:

"Marta Abba's screen debut in "Loyalty of Love"…is promising, but it is not nearly so felicitous an introduction to the charming Italian actress as "Tovarich"….her picture, unlike her play, has been poorly written and wretchedly produced. Handicapped by a dull script, inept direction, bad photography and incoherent editing, Miss Abba emerges triumphantly with an eloquent and touching performance. It is a demonstration all the more remarkable because the role, in itself, is merely a stereotype of wifely devotion…but there are dignity, honesty, and vibrance in her playing, and the screen becomes electric when she fills it….We shall feel better about Miss Abba when Hollywood takes her in hand" (Frank S. Nugent, *New York Times*, March 1, 1937).

It had long been Pirandello's dream that Marta would become a Hollywood superstar. In a letter he wrote to her from Rome on September 25, 1928, for instance, his imagination soars over the news that Marta is learning to drive. He imagines her as a star driving Hollywood's highways of glamour:

> It seems auspicious that you are learning how to drive. Soon in America you'll be driving not an ordinary Ford, but a supercar of a supermaket on the superhighways of Hollywood; you, superstar Marta, queen of the screens of the world! (P, pp. 24-5).

Cars were just then making their way into the Italian imagination; in 1927 Italy held for the first time *The "Mille miglia" (Thousand Miles)*, the most spectacular automobile race in the world, running from Brescia to Rome and back. Right from the start, millions of Italians thronged to watch it and became wildly enthusiastic about cars.

But despite all of Pirandello's best efforts, and despite her own great talents, Hollywood never took to Marta. In the United States, where Pirandello had always imagined great opportunities for both of them, at the age of thirty-six Marta was considered too close to middle age.

Moreover, breaking into the world of American film might have required a radical change in her acting style, which was thoroughly theatrical and idiosyncratic, and this would mean losing her identity as an actress, on which Pirandello had had a formative influence.

It was in the Hollywood of the 1930s that the first great divas emerged, created as incarnations of absolute femininity. For the sake of a style or an idea which they were asked to embody, the actresses submitted to physical alterations: they lost or gained weight, they highlighted their features—sometimes their cheekbones, sometimes their foreheads—and their eyes were made to appear larger with cosmetics and made to look deeper by shading their eyelids. And the long curving line of the eyebrow assumed a knowing and somewhat disturbing look. Thanks to the subtle manipulations not only of make-up artists but also of hairdressers and tailors, these years saw the beginning of the phenomenon, closely linked to the fortunes of the film industry, of the piece-by-piece fabrication of famous femmes fatales. They were the greatest female fetishes of the sound era, the sacred Venuses of the public imagination. Mythical images, which were produced to win over the spectator, took on life. Roland Barthes rightly remarks in *Mythologies*: "Garbo still belongs to that moment in cinema when capturing the human face still plunged audiences into the deepest ecstasy, when one literally lost oneself in a human image as one would in a philtre, when the face represented a kind of absolute state of the flesh, which could be neither reached nor renounced. A few years earlier the face of Valentino was causing suicides; that of Garbo still partakes of the same rule of Courtly Love, where the flesh gives rise to mystical feelings of perdition" (p. 56).

It is not by chance that Garbo was chosen for the screen version of *As You Desire Me* (1932), originally performed on stage by Marta in 1930. Through the many masks of art and movie magic there emerged a haunting and troubled beauty. Garbo was able to express the internal torments of "the Unknown," the play's female protagonist, as perhaps had not been possible even for the best stage actress. Unlike most of Pirandello's plays, which were based on earlier short stories, *As You Desire Me* was based on an event that took place in Italy in 1927, the Bruneri-Canella case, in which an unknown man at the asylum of Collegno, in Turin, was recognized by Giulia Canella as her husband Giulio, a captain in the Italian Army who had disappeared during the First World War. At the same time he was identified by his family as Mario Bruneri, a printer who several years before had been charged with fraud and then disappeared.

But the complex art of visual enhancements that had transformed actresses who had come to Hollywood in the late '20s and early '30s, like Greta Garbo and Marlene Dietrich, did not affect in the slightest the bodily appearance of Marta Abba, who remained firmly bound to theatrical roles once it became clear that the opportunity for comparable film roles would not present itself. Coming to America at age 36 (the same age as Greta Garbo when she began to become more solitary and aloof, concealing her life in a veil of mystery), Marta was perhaps too old to aspire to a similar refashioning. This was not the case with Ingrid Bergman, another European actress, who in 1936 was twenty-one years old and on her way up to the heights of international stardom.

Besides her age and background of stage acting, Marta Abba's fortunes were closely linked to Pirandello's name and works. This was not just because for more than ten years the playwright had a strong and continuous influence on her, but also because, by happy coincidence, her artistic nature and sensibility harmonized perfectly with Pirandello's and were a suitable match for his plots. We might say that by temperament Abba was already a Pirandellian actress, and that perhaps without Pirandello it would have been difficult for her to express herself fully. In fact, as she recalled to me in our conversations, even before she met the playwright in 1925, she knew his earlier plays and liked them very much. She recalled talking with other actors who found his plays and characters difficult, but she herself did not share this impression, feeling instead that his characters were congenial to her own talents and sensibilities. We may wonder, then, whether, even with her exceptional talent, she would have had such success without Pirandello at a time that was growing unpropitious for Pirandello's theater.

For Pirandello himself, despite his authority, had to work hard to battle against misunderstandings, caution, and conformism in a public that was accustomed to enjoy itself while seeing, at best, its own hypocrisies exposed on the stage. The social and psychological analyses of Pirandello's plays were ruthless, and always led to conclusions as true as they were hard to swallow. To dramas of this critical depth, the audience reacted with coarseness and, at times, violence. Harsh critics often led theater-goers to desert his productions en masse. The tragedy of what was depicted on stage was not only an end in itself, but pointed toward an even more tragic future. Marta certainly sensed all of this, but alone it would not have been easy for her to express it. Pirandello came to her aid, making her the ideal interpreter of his thinking and unconsciously compelling her to assume that fixed and inflexible role about which his own *Six Characters* had protested so vividly.

Marta's last letter to the Maestro was written on December 1, 1936. For the first time there was no letter in response, only a telegram sent by her father, which reached her on December 10, bringing the tragic news of Pirandello's sudden death. That very same evening she appeared on the stage of the Plymouth Theater and with a broken voice gave the public the sad news. At the time the actress was performing at the Plymouth Theater on Broadway in Jacques Deval's *Tovarich*. Adapted into English by the famed American playwright Robert E. Sherwood, it was a brilliant comedy about a Russian aristocratic couple who after the Bolshevik Revolution take refuge in Paris, where in order to survive they get jobs as house servants. With Marta in the lead role as the Grand Duchess Tatiana Petrovna, and thanks to her stage experience and the fascination of a voice that enunciated its English with a lilting Russian accent, the comedy was hugely successful. She acted opposite John Halliday, and the show ran for 356 performances. Although the United States is a land of immigrants, Broadway show business has not always been hospitable to foreign talent, save mainly for those born where English is the mother tongue. But Marta won over the New York audience and critics in a single night; her enthusiastic reviewers included Brooks Atkinson of the *New York Times*,

Sidney Carroll of "Stage," and Edith Isaacs of "Arts Monthly." One critic had written after the debut that Marta had "conquered Broadway in one evening."

Before its Broadway premiere, the play had opened in Baltimore, followed by a short run in Philadelphia. Marta wrote to Pirandello in early October, 1936, about her impressions of the show and the local audiences' reactions. "Last night after my debut in Philadelphia I sent you a telegram. I believe there is no other theater more inhospitable nor public colder than this one…" (The Warwick, Philadelphia, Oct. 6, 1936; C, p. 380). But after the second performance the city seems to have warmed to her, and Marta was beginning to get good critical indications of the show's positive reception. On October 8, she wrote that "Even the people of Philadelphia seem to have been reawakened" (C, p. 382). Two days later, she wrote: "My personal success is magnificent […] The Philadelphia critics, known to be very severe, have all been in agreement in their recognition of me. This has made a lot of news and the public is rushing to it" (Oct. 10, 1936; C, p. 385).

But by a strange twist of fate her acting career, which was just taking off in America, came to an end upon Pirandello's death. Now stranded in New York, she came to miss the artistic support of the Maestro, who had always protected her through thick and thin, as is shown by the last letters sent to her right up until a few days before his death, as full of advice and suggestions as ever. Marta Abba felt that the ground had been taken from beneath her feet, particularly in Italy, where after his death she felt she would be unable to return and make any sort of career. As long as the Maestro had been there to follow and guide her movements, even while he was on the other side of the Atlantic, the actress felt contented. Moreover, he had been the one to insist that Marta move, first to England, where he recommended her to J. M. Barrie (the author of *Peter Pan*) and then to the United States, in order to expose her as an actress to a wider view of the world, not only in an artistic sense but economically as well. Marta was also aware that Pirandello's death made her eventual return to the Italian theater scene more difficult. Her career would certainly have been blocked by all those who were hostile to the Maestro, whose drama had shaken theatrical conventions to their foundations. Those who were jealous of her privileged position as Pirandello's protégée, both in his theatrical work and in his private life, would now have an easier time attacking her.

Mrs. Severance A. Millikin

When *Tovarich*'s run came to end, Marta Abba became engaged to Severance A. Millikin, one of the most prominent young scions of Cleveland, Ohio. His family had funded the building of the Cleveland Orchestra, which opened in 1931 with the name of Severance Hall, the first auditorium in the U.S. that was built for live radio broadcasts. The local newspapers announced the marriage, which took place on January 28, 1938, between a man considered one of city's most eligible bachelors and the Italian actress, at which time the couple also announced to the press her plans to withdraw from the public eye. Everything we know about the marriage suggests that it was a search for a safe harbor from a faltering career that had not brought her success in film in America and that in Italy would have had to face substantial hostility. At the same time, the political scene in Europe was succumbing to a more and more belligerent tone.

All the same, it is also possible that in her decision to choose marriage and abandon her career, the fear of the new and the different that suddenly yawned before her with Pirandello's death played an important role. Marta Abba the actress 'died' along with the writer, putting the final seal on the relationship of mutual dependence that was confirmed throughout their lengthy correspondence. Devoted mainly to the interpretation of Pirandellian roles, Marta was reluctant to stray too far from the theatrical techniques that she had learned from Pirandello and that had been her nourishment for eleven full years. Although she had played characters of Shaw, Ibsen, D'Annunzio, and others, and had worked with directors like Max Reinhardt, her artistic choices were still tethered to a vision of the theater that had ripened under the tutelage of the Maestro. This did not allow her to grow as an actress in response to the very different demands and expectations of other writers and directors, and, in particular, to the inflexible rules of the motion picture. She stubbornly wished to remain faithful to these choices, rather than accept an image completely imposed from without that turned the Maestro's schooling upside down. For the sake of coherence with the vision she had of herself and the theater, she preferred to stay loyal to her own choices, for which she always took responsibility and faced the consequences herself. Her public had loved her as a particular type, and she would always remain faithful to her beloved image.

Thus aside from the legal wrangling between Marta Abba and Pirandello's heirs, it is clear that with his death her acting trajectory too reached its nadir. She would now enter into the cocooned life of the wealthy Cleveland upper class, although in her own mind Marta never completely renounced the theater. Her new life as the wife of one of the most prominent men of the city was not without its advantages for an actress who had just lost the one fixed point of reference in her life. She could not avoid the difficult recognition that she was no longer in the first blush of youth. The rarefied atmosphere in 1938 of the American Midwestern elite, which had recovered its fortunes after the catastrophe of 1929 and the worst of the Depression, guaranteed her at any rate a comfortable life, and protected her from the economic uncertainties that would have faced her had she returned to Italy. Unlike Europe, which was now teetering on the edge of disaster, America was enjoying a resurgence of prosperity. Against this new backdrop, the actress could even convince herself that she was still performing. It was an ideal setting, albeit a static one, for a woman who was accustomed to performing. And for a charismatic woman who was used to charming her audience, it was not difficult to attract attention. Moreover, in addition to her charm, Marta won everyone over with her perfect English and only slight foreign accent. In America, then and now, people listen eagerly to those who give an exotic coloration to their grammatically impeccable English.

Very soon, however, Marta Abba began to realize the limitations of this world. The days drew out languorously in a house with little to occupy her. They must have seemed interminable, particularly for one who had been used to traveling continuously from city to city, practicing and performing new roles. Another novelty was the atmosphere of matriarchal rule established by her austere mother-in-law, who dominated the household. For her part, the older woman, with subtle feminine intuition, perhaps understood that it might not be easy for a lady like Marta to get used to their lifestyle. How could an elegant, cosmopolitan Italian woman so different from them adapt herself to that stifling Midwestern life, where the women had their accepted wifely duties, an occasional concert in the local Symphony Hall or exotic vacations to Antigua, and beyond this at most the hope of participating in philanthropic and charitable activities? How far this life must have been in every respect from the itinerant life of show business she had lived for the last decade or more! Even after so many years the actress still vividly remembered the question her mother-in-law used to ask her, trying to discern the state of mind that underlay her daughter-in-law's troubles: "Are you happy, dear?"

Marta was happy—truly happy—at least for a short while, a happiness more sought for than attained. To keep herself active during these years, she became involved in organizing and directing a summer theater program in Cleveland. But the realization of what it meant to live in such a different world and so far from those she had known, the lack of novelty in that upper-crust and suffocating atmosphere, the impossibility of truly identifying herself with the fixed role of wife, must have eventually gotten the upper hand. There began for Marta a time of reconsideration and of nostalgia for long-lost feelings, which the years spent with her husband only caused to slumber. But it was too late. Events had placed Europe off limits. The dark days of the war saw Italy pitted against Marta Abba's host country, and cast a pall over her relations with the society in which she lived—even with her own relatives. As Marta told me, during the war she was, like everybody else, cut off from communicating with her family in Italy. Occasionally, however, thanks to the Millikin family connections, she was able to get through to them through special Red Cross channels.

Her relations with her husband also cooled off further as a result of her relationship with a German housekeeper in the house, a relationship that was fraught with troubling implications. It was probably their status as common 'enemies' of their host country that fostered a feeling of sympathy between them, and that made the housekeeper an intimate confidante of Marta's worries and demons. Their friendship grew closer day by day and became intimate to the point of shutting out everyone else.

This was not an isolated episode of 'close female friendship' for the actress, as Marta also formed a devoted friendship with an heiress, Mildred Putnam, that would continue after her divorce and return to Italy in 1953. Mrs. Putnam took her into her home during the difficult divorce proceedings, while Marta was still living in Cleveland, and offered her consolation, expecting faithful friendship in return. That, thirty years later, Mrs. Putnam would be the one to suggest to Marta that she donate her correspondence with Pirandello to Princeton University, the *alma mater* of her sons John and Peter Putnam (and, incidentally, of Severance Millikin as well), implies how close the relationship was until Mrs. Putnam's death in the spring of 1984. Her sons had graduated from Princeton in 1945 and 1946 respectively, and following this Mrs. Putnam retained close ties to the university, particularly through the Putnam Foundation, which over the years has made generous donations of artistic and cultural works to Princeton and other institutions.

Divorce

Severance Millikin first filed a petition for divorce and equitable relief on September 16, 1950, in Cuyahoga County, Ohio. Marta filed a counter-petition for divorce and alimony on October 20, 1950. Hearings were held in late 1951, and were apparently messy. All manner of financial records were subpoenaed—bank statements, commercial checks and stubs, years of back tax return records, profit and loss statements, financial ledgers and journals, etc. The plaintiff, for his part, charged that "the defendant has been guilty of gross neglect of duty toward the plaintiff." The public records I obtained from the Cleveland Clerk of Courts do not, unfortunately, expand on what Mr. Millikin might have been implying, or what he might have stated in court testimony—what substance, in short, was implied by "gross neglect of duty."

Marta's counter-petition is more substantive, and makes clear that her chief concern was to obtain alimony in order to have a means of support in the absence of the support provided by the marriage.

> Defendant further says that she has always conducted herself as a good and dutiful wife toward the plaintiff and that at all times she has performed the marital duties and obligations incumbent upon her to perform, but that the plaintiff, in disregard of his marital duties and obligations, has been guilty of gross neglect of duty and extreme cruelty and has abandoned the defendant without cause.

> The above action filed by the Plaintiff is for a divorce. The Defendant denies the divorce and does not want one, but she is entitled to have *the question of their marital relations* permanently established [emphasis added]. The Defendant has not taken the time of the Court to establish for herself, adequate and sufficient support, *pendente lite*, or attorneys fees and has held such items in abeyance, hoping that the Court would reach this case for trial prior to this time. Consequently, she has been inadequately supported and many questions of her support and family economies have led to further misunderstandings and humiliations.

> The Defendant, through the past year has suffered great distress of having an unjust divorce action pending against her and feels that a determination of this question and the question of support, maintenance and alimony for herself

would relieve her mental anguish caused by the pendency of this unfair action. This Defendant has been married to the Plaintiff for fourteen years and prior to said marriage, enjoyed a very valuable and esteemed reputation as an artist, performing in outstanding plays, both in continental Europe and in the United States; that she gave up her profession, her career and her highly paid compensation as an outstanding actress for marriage with the Plaintiff, and has been a loyal and faithful wife, but believes now that after a pendency of this action for a period of one year, she is entitled to have these questions immediately determined by a trial of the issues involved therein (Divorce records case number 618219, Mr. and Mrs. Severance A. Millikin, file date 9-16-1950).

Reading between the lines, one cannot help but suspect that sexual matters are behind the oblique legal phrase "marital duties and obligations." Again, no additional evidence that might shed light on the marital dispute is forthcoming. But the phrase further down in the laconic legal narrative, "the Defendant…is entitled to have the question of their marital relations permanently established," is also suggestive of the same idea—namely, that the husband was in some way impugning his wife's behavior in the bedroom. Did Marta spurn her husband's sexual affections? Did her husband know, or suspect something of Marta's close intimacies with the German housekeeper, or some other girlfriend? It is impossible to tell. We may never know more than what can be known from these divorce records. The rest is mere speculation. There is just one more small detail I can add from my conversations with Marta. She told me once that at the trial the German housekeeper was called as a witness and "betrayed" her. I did not ask in what way, and Marta did not elaborate.

The final hearing on the divorce was held and settled on Feb. 4, 1952. Marta was apparently more persuasive before the court than her husband, because the court decided in her favor, finding that "the plaintiff has been guilty of gross neglect of duty toward the defendant as alleged in said amended cross petition, and that by reason thereof the defendant is entitled to a divorce as prayed for."

The record notes that the parties entered into an agreement to settle, concerning alimony and property rights, that was found to be "fair, just and equitable," and that the agreement had been executed. Thus the divorce was officially granted. Nevertheless, for unknown reasons the matter came to court again in September 1955, regarding an unstated amendment of the settlement agreement of Feb. 1952. Thus, for a marriage of fourteen years, Marta endured a divorce that itself lasted five.

Impossible Loves

There are two contemporary accounts of the relationship between Pirandello and Marta Abba, both of which are worth citing. Paola Masino, a writer of the time familiar with the couple, reported:

> I met Marta Abba in 1925, the same year Pirandello met her. I know this much: there were never physical relations between Marta Abba and Pirandello. Marta was a young maiden for him, and was to remain so until she married. Pirandello loved her, but in his own way, and she may have chafed at this...Pirandello was of a strict morality. He could not stand the thought of betrayal between man and wife, between lovers...one evening we were in a restaurant at Sanremo when a lady came in, the wife of a journalist. It was known that this lady was cheating on her husband. I knew the woman, we had attended the same school. Pirandello barked at me: 'Don't say hello. One doesn't acknowledge such women.' It was she who came over and said hello to me. I had to answer. He got furious and repeated, loudly, so that she would hear, 'One doesn't greet that kind of woman' ("Pirandello e il *Corriere* 1876-1986," p. 31).

Secondly, there was the highly personal preface to Pirandello's *Short Stories for a Year* written by Corrado Alvaro, another of Pirandello's close friends. This extraordinary preface was cut from the Mondadori edition of the work, having been the object of a judicial procedure brought by Marta Abba's lawyers, as containing "slanderous insults against [Pirandello's] moral and artistic character," after a Milan Court of Appeals, in a decision of July 2, 1965, had handed down a sentence prohibiting its reprinting. Alvaro embellished his 'memories' of events in his usual masterly fashion:

> [...] Looking into his [personal] desk drawer, I found a yellowed piece of paper on which he [Pirandello] confessed the end of his youth, that his body was ravaged by time, and therefore the end of physical love. He was marking a precise point: it was the time when as a man he could no longer give more joy than he will receive...Therefore, perhaps, he took on the role in his last years of one who can give that which he knows is a gift: warm, unstinting friendship and admiration, his protection and the benefit of his experience (p. 12).

As we can see, these are the impressions of people who knew Pirandello well, who came to discern not only his moralism, but also some of his frailties, and perhaps even his passions. But it is open to doubt how far they could recognize the torments in the writer's soul, when at the age of 62 the fire of his love for Marta made his body tremble with pleasure, mastered, as he himself says, by the "beast." Pirandello suffered from insomnia, but, in a letter quoted earlier that bears repeating here, he writes: "I make an effort to sleep, forbidding myself to think, to feel; I cannot; the body does not want to; the beast does not get tired and, although whipped it still does not want to; maybe it conceals a disease that I don't know about yet; but if it cannot help itself, I certainly can't" (Berlin, April 8, 1929; P, p. 64).

The letters he wrote to the actress provide only partial answers to these questions, which have left the field open to decades of endless conjecture and debate. The reports of Masino and Alvaro are important, yet they remain only opinions emerging out of social and professional relations. They have nevertheless been taken by some as ironclad testimony to a secret love affair between Pirandello and Marta Abba. Although these witnesses are important to us, reflecting the reality that they knew, they were clearly unaware of Marta's feelings about her relationship with Pirandello throughout this period. But we do know from some of Marta's replies to his letters that every reference by Pirandello to his love made her profoundly uncomfortable.

Pirandello and Marta Abba did indeed have a love story, with him clearly experiencing physical desire for her, as the quotations cited earlier make clear. But it is also the story of an impossible love, which was all the more real and dramatic because it was transferred to the world of absolutes of which the literary realm consists. Marta's letters to Pirandello reveal all of this, along with their theatrical affairs, their struggles, their hopes, and their moments of candor. But above all the correspondence attests to the deep relationship, lived in the love of art and in a kind of sublimated transference, which shifts the impossibility of realizing a merely erotic love into the regions of the sublime and the absolute.

Their 'love story,' however, must have been greatly oversimplified in the rumors that circulated at the time. The letters even gave rise to a challenge to a duel, conducted with proper ceremony, which was to pit Marta's father against a certain Zopegni, who apparently made disparaging remarks in public about the actress and 'her' playwright. Pirandello for his part constantly tried to protect her more than himself, as she was suffering more in reputation than he from their association. The story had begun in the 1920s, when the mere suspicion of a relationship such as existed between the writer (still legally bound to his wife) and the actress would be enough to lay all guilt at the woman's feet, penalizing her without mercy. Marta Abba was, by sex and by profession, doubly handicapped. In the case of a man, and especially an old and celebrated man, public opinion was far more inclined to be tolerant. It was up to her to wash away the blame. And so she did. "Friends," the actress bitterly recalled to me,

Abandoned me on the death of the Maestro, I was left alone;

they were concerned only with exploiting their friendship with the Maestro. When I asked for help, no one wanted to help, on the contrary, they were against me, opposing my return to the theater. Even my films disappeared from view: when I asked where they had wound up, they told me they had been lost. Luckily, I was able to get back the letters I had written to the Maestro. When he died I was in the United States, but my poor Dad went to the funeral in Rome, and there he found all of these so-called friends (Bontempelli, Alvaro and the rest) in quite a lighthearted mood, which was inappropriate for the pain felt at the sudden and premature loss of the Maestro. Dad went back to Milan, disappointed and embittered; but he was able to recover for me all the letters I had written in those many years. I was excluded from everything from then on. His 'friends,' who had, perhaps only for the sake of politeness or awe for the Maestro, accepted me for all those years, did everything they could to banish me and see that I was utterly forgotten. I therefore decided to continue working in America, where the Maestro had always wanted me to go…

The actress told me all of these things while maintaining a penetrating gaze, as if to see how much her interlocutor could understand her anguish, which she re-lived with the vivid force of a woman who was able to cope with the many blows she had suffered and yet always remain faithful to herself and to her career as an actress.

Marta never met her soul mate, man or woman. Her love life was more like a long sequence of brief flames and infatuations. She had in fact been engaged in the early 1920s to a young man from Genoa, but she ended it after a few months. Although she was a very reserved woman, sometimes a little misanthropic, sometimes a bit misogynistic, she loved women passionately, even as she despised them, and she tried to love men as well. In her twenties she was tall, slightly androgynous, and good looking, but without the typical features of feminine beauty. Her gaze was intense, and her auburn hair had reddish tones. One friend who probably realized her sexual tendencies was Mildred Putnam, with whom she became very close while she lived as Mrs. Millikin in America. Mildred was probably one of her forbidden soul mates, among whom is also the "blonde professor" (as Marta always called her) of Columbia University, with whom she became very close after her divorce. Marta had moved to New York City and founded the Pirandello Society, beginning work on translations of some of Pirandello's plays into English. In the 1980s, the same professor invited me to speak at Columbia on the then-unpublished correspondence between Pirandello and Abba, and at that time she confided in me that Marta had courted her strongly and tried her best to seduce her, though she rejected Marta's overtures.

Life became more difficult for Marta after her divorce from Millikin. Her disappointments and social instability made her more tormented and isolated. In her sixties, the desolation became palpable in her manner, and uneasiness and disappointment were even visible in her physical appearance. In the 1960s and much of the 1970s she divided her time between her Tuscan estate in Fauglia, Pisa, which she called *Trovarsi* (and where she had a small theater where students from the University of Pisa would produce plays under her direction) and her condominium in Monte Carlo. However, in the 80s after she sold *Trovarsi*, she divided her time between Monte Carlo and Milan, where she lived with her sister Cele at their condominium on Via Regina Giovanna. When I met her there in February, 1984, I was saddened by her appearance. She was not the Marta Abba I had expected. Communicating with her was not simple. One had to be very patient with her sudden silences and her suspiciousness; she was a true master of making people feel uneasy.

"After I realized what they were doing to my career, I wanted to confront some people, but I realized that it was totally worthless, so I held my tongue," Marta told me on one occasion. Marta was referring to the antagonistic complex of personal relations and professional critics that had dogged her career since the 1920s, but which became far more pronounced upon her return to Italy in 1953. The hostilities that resurfaced would plague Marta for years to come, but they had deep roots in her past with the Maestro, centering especially on his family's dislike for the actress, and their constantly frustrated attempts to sever ties with Marta after Pirandello's death.

Marta's Bitter Homecoming

After the protracted divorce that awarded her over a million dollars—a vast sum in the early 1950s—as compensation for the acting career she had given up upon marrying, Marta Abba returned permanently to Italy. But it proved to be a bitter homecoming for several reasons, in particular because her presence reignited an old conflict with Pirandello's heirs. At the same time she had to face the ire of old enemies and false friends who emerged out of the shadows of her past. To understand what happened, it is best to recall the state of things in Italy before Marta had left.

The correspondence speaks eloquently on the many difficulties Pirandello and Marta faced in their theatrical work. Their deep passion for their art drove them in search of a more sophisticated form of theatrical representation, toward a more original repertoire, one open to interpretations and freed from the constraints of conventional norms. It is precisely for this reason that they ended up clashing with certain critics, above all Silvio d'Amico, who at that time was considered among the most authoritative drama critics. D'Amico always boasted that he was open to novelties and change, but in fact he tended only to accept 'novelties' that were closely tied to traditional canons. One of these conventions apparently stipulated that the actress, even if she was already over thirty (Marta had begun her career when still in her teens), was still too young to play the leading lady. In accordance with this judgment, Marta was accused of having never completed a sufficient period of training, and even of never having had real teachers. But what about Pirandello, who not only wrote plays expressly for her but also worked closely with her on acting and performing the characters? It was this that had made her into an actress widely recognized as 'Pirandellian,' even though she had successfully performed plays by other authors (Goldoni, H. Mann, Shaw, Shakespeare, d'Annunzio).

But this versatility was not enough to placate the hostility of those critics who never missed an opportunity to disparage her. Attacks by critics were often so heavy-handed and severe that their objectivity seems doubtful, and one wonders about their ulterior motives. How could it be, for instance, that at the peak of her career, in her early thirties and capable of expressing herself on stage with extraordinary intensity and passion, she would be considered too young and inexperienced for a leading role, when she had already performed brilliantly for years on many of the best stages in Europe and South America? Not to mention that only a few years later, she would be recognized by the most important American critics for her performances on Broadway.

But d'Amico's critical attitude toward Marta rarely, if ever, gave her any credit for her talents or achievements. On April 1, 1931, for example, after a performance in Rome of *As You Desire Me*, d'Amico wrote in the *Tribuna* that Marta's diction was "drawn out and lamentatious, lacking any skill of tone, without nuance, without any logical or lyrical force." But what the critic described as lacking nuance and logic was actually a more modern style—called *respiro corto* (short breath) and *ansimante* (gasping)—which she had learned in 1924 before she met Pirandello, while performing Chekhov's *Seagull*, her first dramatic success. One might find this 'drawn out' style of delivery enjoyable or not, and consider it either a virtue or defect. In Marta's case d'Amico decided it was a defect. But this judgment must be seen for the subjective criticism it is, since the history of theater and cinema offers many examples of actors and actresses whose idiosyncratic delivery styles are key elements in their popularity and mythic allure.

But such critics were expressing in veiled terms other moral judgments that were less appropriate to voice in public. Marta's 'friendship' with Pirandello was always a source of gossip, especially in Rome where his family lived, and in time they developed ties of marriage with the d'Amico family, with the two families becoming very close. Moreover, in the Italian world of show business she had also become a target of jealousy because of her being the 'Pirandellian' actress. Why was she the one to have such a privileged relationship with the great playwright? No one dared to speak about these matters openly, and yet the two were most certainly, though implicitly, judged. We can feel this judgment even in Marta's letters, although only in vague and discrete traces, and it was quite destructive in its effects. If their relationship was one that had limits that were difficult to define, it appeared all the more disquieting because it could not be labeled within the usual terms of ethics and etiquette. It was easier merely to brand her a 'Pirandellian' actress, and a term that might have expressed a positive judgment instead became a stigma loaded with much more ambiguity. All of this perhaps underlay the moralizing criticisms of Silvio d'Amico (it is no accident that Marta and Pirandello spoke of him as "that priest"), who, when not daring to attack the playwright openly, would instead aim the devastating arrows of his critiques at his actress. Marta was the more vulnerable of the two, firstly because she was an actress, a profession still somewhat of ill repute, and secondly because she was a woman.

It was far easier, therefore, for d'Amico to attack her character under the guise of merely fulfilling his critical duties in the name of art. Also working against her, and placing her in a precarious situation, was that the actress, who was so charming on stage, in real life scrupulously avoided using her femininity to 'seduce' and charm her critics. Moreover, the mental and moral tension that Marta managed to project toward those with whom she dealt, along with her natural pride, was far removed from the obsequious docility that actresses generally showed—or were expected to show—to their critics. This irritated most of them, who were used to quite different behavior.

The lofty views she held of the theater as an expression of pure and original art were not the main source of conflict with critics, whose mediocrity and dishonest dealings she never hesitated to point out. Such critics, feeling judged by her penetrating gaze, which was capable of laying bare their thinly veiled motives and the excuses they used to hide their scheming questions, singled her out and created difficulties for her. Aggravating this already difficult situation were some who treated her in bad faith, manipulating and cheating her. It was partly for these reasons that the actress had decided to leave Italy for America in the first place, casting behind her the shadows that such conflicts project, and making it difficult to define the margins between victim and oppressor, guilt and innocence, truth and lies.

Such had been the state of things before Marta left. Now, upon her return to Italy, she found herself once again in these hostile waters. In Marta's mind, the chief source of the conflict was the actions and attitudes of Pirandello's heirs, and here we do not have to search far to discover the reasons for the systematic animosity toward Marta. After Pirandello's death, his family inherited his estate. Marta was in the United States, and the family claimed that there had been no will. But several years after Pirandello's death, Marta's sister Cele found a will that he had hidden in one of the books at their house to circumvent Marta's objections to being included in it. In it, Pirandello stipulated that Marta should be treated like one of his children. The document became an official part of the estate record in the 1950s, and the basis of a long and bitter legal dispute that played out between Marta and the Pirandello family (which had become through marriage part of the powerful d'Amico dynasty). Marta recounted to me in conversation:

> Scheming critics and old enemies of the Maestro set their faces against me, especially when I came back, alone, from America, and decided to make a comeback in the theater. Those who might have helped me, either with favorable reviews, or by inviting me to work in television, which in the Fifties had just started to take off, were hand in glove with Pirandello's heirs, who have been against me all my life; especially after I brought a suit against them, once I found the will Pirandello had drawn up for me many years before, which I had refused at the time, left forgotten in a book. The Maestro had written in that

document that I was to be considered like one of his daughters. As you know, the suit ended with a verdict that offered me the rights to the last nine plays he had written. Those red pen marks are clear reminders of the action, which underline the parts in which the Maestro refers to the cooperative role I played in the writing of some of the plays written in the last ten years of his life.

In other words, Marta became almost like a curse to the family. The 'other woman,' whom they had always more or less openly despised, did not go away or disappear from their lives with the death of their father. They would most likely have preferred to forget about Marta, to never have to see or think about her again. But the stipulation in the will that she receive the rights to nine plays made such an outcome totally impossible. Like it or not, she was a co-heir to Pirandello's precious literary estate. Nevertheless, his granddaughter Maria Luisa Aguirre d'Amico, Lietta Pirandello's daughter, has seen to it over the years that Marta be erased from the 'official memory' of the great playwright Luigi Pirandello as much as possible.

Pirandello Family Troubles

The chronic ill will between Marta Abba and Pirandello's family at first had nothing to do with Marta. It was, rather, a manifestation of the difficulties Pirandello had been having within his own family, especially with his daughter Lietta, problems that began well before he met Marta. With his wife's persistent psychological instability, Lietta had been the surrogate woman of the house ever since she had been a teenager, even appearing in public with her father at major events. At the 1921 premiere in Rome of *Six Characters*, for instance, it was Lietta and not her mother (who was already in an asylum) who accompanied the playwright. That same year Lietta married a young man, Manuel Aguirre, (a military attaché at the Vatican) and moved to his native Chile. But soon after her father met

A Star is (Not Quite) Born

Marta in 1925 Lietta returned to Italy, at which point a crisis that had been mounting between Lietta and her father came to a head. It remains partly shrouded in mystery, but it involved Lietta and her husband's use, even squandering, of the Pirandello family assets.

Thanks to the recent publication of several of Pirandello's letters to Lietta (under the care of Lietta's daughter Maria Luisa) many details of the story have become clear. Pirandello was at first content enough with his daughter's husband. He regarded him as a "man of honor," as he says in several letters, and treated him with a fatherly affection in the letters. But he was not pleased with the couple's departure to Chile, and apparently Manuel had given Pirandello his word that their trip would be short, at most a year or eighteen months. But news from Lietta in Chile of Manuel's desire to buy farmland there soon made her father doubt both Manuel's intentions and his character. Pirandello wanted Lietta home. He wrote to her on April 14, 1922:

> I need, need you to return at once, my little daughter, if you don't want me to die of this anguish for which I can find no relief. I entrusted you to a man of honor, whose word that he gave me I hold as sacred, when he said that he would do everything to bring you back to Italy as soon as possible. (*Lettere a Lietta*, p. 32)

This family drama soon reached a crisis point, and the grievances were articulated in Pirandello's letters to Lietta over the next several months. Money was always the major sticking point. Pirandello had agreed to establish as a dowry for Lietta an account interest on which would go to Lietta on a monthly basis. Nevertheless, strange and urgent telegrams began to arrive from Chile, always requesting more money. The issue came to a head when Lietta's first child, Manolo, was born, a sickly son who, sadly, would die in 1925. In the same letter congratulating her on the child's birth, Pirandello revealed to his daughter in the most candid terms what he had come to think of her husband:

The news that you are in need of my financial help for your care has so distressed and upset me that my last letters have been from start to finish a violent fuming of my bitterness and my distress...Know, my little Lietta, that my indignation is justified by *precise facts and figures* that I have—and that I can relate to you when you wish—from which it has become most evident that your husband—out of greed—or for something else I know not what—has wanted to inflict a martyr's death upon me, and this will not cease until the day you are returned to me; with the further result for him that he has lost all trust on my part in his word. I know, transaction by transaction, all the money that he has received; I know what he *really* paid for the trip (and not what, lying, he told me and made you believe), I know what his real expenses were while in Rome; and I am *certain* (unless he lost the money gambling or has thrown it away) that he has deliberately had the cruelty of making you, my dear daughter, abuse your father from afar, that also I gave him such proofs of good will and prudent care, with this martyr's death of knowing you are in a foreign country in the hands of a man in such need, who cannot give you help—and this *without being true*. I forgive everything, today, for the birth of your innocent son; and you too, my little Lietta, don't think of all this...After all that has happened, with the *certainty* I have acquired, I cannot leave you there alone with him. I could have left you there for some time, while I trusted him. But now that I have lost it all, as well as the cost of supporting you and your child, you must return to me at once (May 24, 1922; original emphasis, pp. 41-2).

Several things become clear from this unhappy letter and the mounting crisis that unfolds in those that follow it. First of all, it bears repeating that this family unraveling occurred three full years before Marta met Pirandello. She entered his life unaware of this unpleasant family situation, and bore no responsibility for its awkward and painful outcome. Secondly, these letters also make clear something that is important to understanding the author's relationship with Marta: Pirandello treated his daughter with a tender and loving affection—indeed bordering on obsessive—and he uses precisely the same rhetorical language and emotional ploys with her that will become the norm in his correspondence with Marta. It would seem that after his falling out with Lietta and her husband and upon his meeting the actress, Pirandello rather quickly transferred his emotional complexes from his daughter to Marta, and began subjecting her to his same routines of love, guilt, and psychological control.

But to finish the story of Pirandello and his daughter: telegrams and letters continued to arrive, urgently requesting and demanding money from Pirandello for the young family's needs in Chile. He was deeply troubled by these requests. "Isn't it enough torture to know you are far away? Also the torture of knowing you are in need? No, no, it is too much, too much! I am fed up! This torture must end!" (May 28, 1922), he says in one. "I still cannot understand these urgent telegrams that I have received with their compulsive requests for money!" (p. 43), he says in another. And again he expresses his angst at her absence and apparent need: "So many times I feel I am swallowed up by the emptiness that surrounds me and is also inside me, that I despair, and I spend terrible moments here alone, in the evening, on the small terrace of the entryway, with my eyes on the stars of the Bear above my head" (June 11, 1922, p. 47).

By the end of June he was fed up. After a letter from Lietta's husband asking for huge sums of money, including an outrageous 5,000 lira to pay for clothes Lietta had had made, he erupts with a bitter image describing his son-in-law:

> he is like a squid that vomits the black ink it has inside it, in moments of rage or desperation....How black, how black, my little Lietta! My soul has been completely stained....I look most of all at the moral aspects: at the spirit he has displayed, at the lies he speaks, at the shame he has not felt to write to a father like me in the way that he has written (June 26, 1922, p. 51).

The letter goes on, in tones no less severe, about her husband's exasperating way of asking for money but providing no news of Lietta and the baby in his letters. His anger and frustration have nearly reached a breaking point: "Do you know what will happen? Once my capacity to suffer has reached its fill, I will fall into a state of apathetic indifference.... All of you will weep and moan and I won't even turn my head to look at you, because you've already made me an idiot from what you have made me suffer. I can't take anymore! I can't take anymore!" (p. 51). Then, after further calling into question Manuel's plans for making a living, and his intentions when he married Lietta, the father in Pirandello cuts to the heart of the matter: "With what courage did he marry you? That I would dress you and buy you shoes with your dowry without costing him anything?" (p. 52).

Thus, in the summer of 1922, relations in the Pirandello family had sunk perilously low. The published correspondence ceases at the end of April, 1923 (resuming in 1931), and things show little sign of improvement by then. The letters continue to focus on money, and to have little good to say about Manuel (usually referred to as "he" or "that man"). Pirandello wires the couple 5,000 lira, and is exasperated in several letters that he has not heard whether they ever received it. Before the published letters end abruptly, there is discussion of the couple coming to live in Italy, where Manuel will be "completely free to come and go as he pleases" (March 31, 1923, p. 89), and Lietta will—revealingly of the way family affairs stood before she married—"have the administration of everything, as you had before" (p. 89).

Early in 1925, the couple, along with their ailing son, did finally return to Italy. It was at the same time that Pirandello was meeting, and no doubt beginning to nourish his peculiar romantic-paternal love for, Marta Abba. It would seem that Lietta was not pleased with this new situation. Indeed, in her memoir *Vivere con Pirandello* [Living with Pirandello], Maria Luisa Aguirre d'Amico relates concerning her mother's return to Italy that at that time she was "jealous, jealous of the woman who took her place and does everything in her power to distance her. In April or May of 1926 she writes a letter to her father which arouses his resentment" (p. 133). Pirandello's granddaughter is of course referring here, in elusive terms, to Marta Abba, with whom the author was spending more and more time, and to the unfortunate events that would end up severing ties for several years between father and daughter.

Piecing together the events hinges, as always, on letters. In this case, however, several key letters, and certain passages of others, were unfortunately suppressed from publication by Pirandello's granddaughter (all letters from August, 1926). But despite this editorial censorship the main outline of the unhappy events is clear.

In these several letters in August Pirandello, at times distraught, at times furious, relates sordid events of his household, which he says had been "a stage for savage quarrels between my sons and my son-in-law" (Rome, August 5, 1926; P, p. 7). The author reveals to Marta that his son-in-law has been manipulating his finances, wildly exaggerating all of his and Lietta's expenses and charging them to Pirandello. In a letter a week later, he says that frauds and betrayals "by the dozens" have been coming to light. Lietta and her husband had disappeared—nobody knew where—taking with them large sums of his royalty payments, as well as his wife's jewelry. He discovers that a piece of land had been purchased with his money but under their name, which he then promptly bought back, also revoking Lietta's power of attorney. A week later he still has no idea where the couple has run off to. Pirandello is in deep distress, both because of the depths of the betrayal he has suffered, and because his finances, which were recently so well off, have now been reduced nearly to nothing overnight.

Finally, on August 20, 1926 Pirandello writes to Marta and refers to a "horrible night" in Como (P, p. 11). This "horrible night spent in Como" has become an infamous piece of Pirandelliana, not least because of the hypothesis that I put forward in my 1991 book, *A Marta Abba per non morire* [To Marta Abba, in order not to die] suggesting that there had been some failed romantic incident in Como that caused the author terrible embarrassment. In the absence of additional revealing evidence, at the time

I proposed a connection between the "horrible night" and the events in one of Pirandello's novels, *Giustino Roncella nato Boggiòlo* (*Giustino Roncella, né Boggiòlo*), originally published in 1911 under the title *Suo marito* (*Her Husband*), then withdrawn from circulation. In 1931, Pirandello began to revise the novel.

In the novel a famous old writer, Maurizio Gueli, while tormented by a woman crazy with jealousy (Pirandello's wife easily comes to mind), falls in love with a beautiful young writer, Silvia Roncella, who is an emerging talent in the theater. Their meeting is magical, a romantic moment of recognition that each is what the other has been searching for in life. But they also both know that there is a terrible and fatal need to express the disquieting desires of the flesh. Why should there be, as part of the love joining two spirits exalted by art, this inevitable horror of making love? The tensions of friendship and sexuality that run through this novel are also basic to the anxieties that run throughout Pirandello's letters to Marta and, in reaction, her letters to him. The romance between Gueli and Silvia ends badly, when it shipwrecks on a single failed embrace one night in Ostia, an awkward, embarrassing embrace, the memory of which torments Silvia right to the end of the novel:

> Among the flashes of smothering images, she still felt her flesh burn with shame for the single embrace, attempted almost coldly, out of a terrible, inevitable necessity there in Ostia, and left desperately incomplete. She would feel sullied by it forever, more than if she had sinned thousands of times with all those young men rumored to have been her lovers. The cloying memory of that single inconclusive embrace had aroused an invincible nausea, a loathing in which every desire for love would be forever drowned (p. 226).

It was with this literary ending in mind that I once put forward the idea that a real-life failed attempt at intimacy between Pirandello and Marta lay behind the mysterious "horrible night" in Como.

Given the entire context of events, however—not least considering the substance of the letters quoted above—I am now much more inclined to think that it was his family's financial troubles that caused the horrible night in Como. Rather than some romantic rejection for which there is no evidence, it is much more plausible to suppose that while in Como, returning from a performance one evening, he received the—infamously 'vanished'—letter Lietta had written him (which she wrote in her two brothers' names as well). In it she refers to rumors circulating in Rome about his relationship with Marta, and also vents her steam about the displacement of her position of control in the house. Lietta, filled with venom about her displacement, convinced her brothers to form a common front in composing this letter, which, read by Pirandello, may have caused him to spend that "horrible night." This letter was the beginning of an escalation of revenge by Lietta and her husband. For how better could she get her revenge than by taking as much of her father's possessions as she could, including money and her mother's jewelry, to punish him and to eliminate any possibility that what had always been hers could ever be lost by passing to the other woman—Marta Abba?

Again, this letter has mysteriously disappeared. But letters written before this time indicate that Lietta and her husband had sent him word that their prodigal spending had finally brought them to bankruptcy, a disaster that seriously strained relations with her father. The letter "written in April or May" that supposedly provoked Pirandello's resentment could well have reached him while he was in Como, since we know that the Teatro d'Arte was performing in Como from the 11th to the 21st of May, 1926. In her account of things Aguirre d'Amico is very circumspect, claiming the letter cannot be found among her mother's papers. On the other hand, she quotes a rough draft of another letter, which she says may or may not have been sent:

> Daddy, maybe you don't care to know how things have been going and are going around here: you have separated yourself even as far as practical matters go and you have to judge without seeing or knowing, based on what you receive up there. So you won't ever know how and why and with what

aim I wrote that letter. I knew that I was defending my Dad and I was blind to all else: the way I did it seemed to me the best, perhaps the only one. Daddikins, you are the only person who made my disgraceful life happy for a few years. But my affection for you no longer matters to you and so you refuse to find excuses for me. I went to Milan to look for you, to tell you what I can't possibly write, but I couldn't find out where you were (*Vivere con Pirandello*, May 11-21, 1926; p. 134).

Put in context, Lietta's jealousy of Marta here is palpable, though it is suppressed and transferred into expressions of abandonment by her father, into claims that he has deserted "practical matters," and into defensive reflexes that she only has him and his interests in mind. In the information supplied by Aguirre d'Amico in lieu of the missing letters, she claims that the supposed disappearance of large sums of money was due to vast amounts spent by Pirandello himself, both to build the villino (detached house) of Via Panvinio, and to cover the great losses incurred by his company during its tour, the financial extremities of which he did not realize.

The interpretation that Pirandello's granddaughter gives the letter from his daughter seems to gibe strangely with the jealousy that she herself acknowledges was affecting Lietta at this time. She instead reads the letter as communicating the slanderous talk of others about the playwright, and Lietta's intemperate attempts at defense. Elsewhere, Aguirre d'Amico's discussion of the events at this time is equally veiled and problematic. In the introduction to her 1979 book *Album di famiglia di Luigi Pirandello* [Luigi Pirandello's Family Album], for instance, Pirandello's granddaughter relates that in 1926:

> following the discord between father and daughter, concerning the construction of the villino, Lietta—my mother—went back to Chile…which for her was always a path of exile. This time Pirandello will not write to his daughter, as he had four years before, after her first departure

to South America: 'My house seems empty, like my life. I need you to return, to return soon my little beauty Lillinetta; if not your papa will die of grief' (20).

In the briefest of terms, without further explanation, the discord is attributed to the "construction of the villino"; the episode is then brushed over with appeals to sentiment and pathos. Following this she is content to leave the matter as an unsolved mystery: "Yes, the unanswered questions are many. What remains perhaps is the regret that by now it is too late to get inside the persons, situations, and moods of Pirandello, his family, his world. Stefano, Lietta, and Fausto have left us no indications, no traces" (21).

Without the letter that would explain the course of events, we are only ever told what Lietta's own daughter thinks, and never the facts of the matter. Naturally, any daughter would want to protect the image of her mother—and not so much that of her grandfather, in this case a sacred figure of international fame whom no accusation could ever harm—and therefore we must accept this 'necessity.' But in this context, when we consider the grave implications and effects that this crisis had on the lives of the three people directly involved (Pirandello, Lietta, and Marta), these events that severed ties between father and daughter were hardly inconsequential.

Thus we may begin increasingly to suspect that the missing letter is the key to understanding this episode, and would explain the "terrible night in Como" to which Pirandello refers. Something in Aguirre d'Amico's account of the situation does not quite fit as far as the letters written during Pirandello's time in Como are concerned. She is always willing to concede that their relationship was strained, but entirely unwilling to delve into the possible, or even plausible, reasons for it. The feud is only ever mentioned in the briefest possible terms before she moves onto other things. And it is for this reason that the 'disappearance' of the relevant letter raises the greatest suspicion. Among the most disturbing mysterious details is the daughter's fruitless search for her father in Milan to tell him "what I am incapable of telling you in writing." What was she so desperate to tell her father that she rushed all the way to Milan to tell him in person? She probably knew or thought that her father was in the area of Milan—Como is only 25 miles from Milan—and news must have reached him somehow (perhaps through Marta's family?). The fact is that Lietta must have realized through Pirandello's reaction that looking for him in Milan must have greatly upset her father, since she apologetically refers to "what I am incapable of telling you in writing."

Luckily enough, the first letter we have from Marta to Pirandello sheds some light on this family misfortune. Writing on August 8, 1926 from Milan, she says that "after nine long days, I have received your letter, which truly pained me." Along with the fact that for Pirandello to leave off writing to the actress for nine days indicates an unusual tumult in his house, Marta's extended reaction to what he has told her provides precious insight into the author's evidently desperate situation:

> Even in your own house you had to be betrayed! If I did not know you were so strong in spirit, and that the storm is largely past, I would be more concerned for you. But I know you, and this reassures me. You still have twenty days to put things in order personally. I hope you can arrange things as well as possible for you and for your children (Milan, 8 August 1926; C, p. 29).

"Even in your own house you had to be betrayed!" Marta's choice of words speaks volumes, for it reveals a crucial fact. Whatever the details of what actually happened in Rome—to the family's vanishing revenues, and with Lietta and Manuel—it is clear that Pirandello himself felt that he had been wronged by a family member, or Marta would never have responded to him in such strong terms about his "betrayal."

This first of the actress' letters also shows that Pirandello had already transferred his psychological attachments to Marta. In his hour of need, she is the one he writes to and confides in. She is the one to whom he unburdens his soul in the long and passionate prose that is now so familiar. And, more importantly, Marta's impassioned response of sympathy and pity indicates that—at least in part—she has become attached to Pirandello as well. He has pulled her in. She is on the way to becoming 'his' actress.

A Star is (Not Quite) Born

The published letters from Pirandello to Lietta end suddenly in 1923 and do not resume until 1931. When they do, the most common issue is once again money. But the tone of the letters has changed, albeit subtly. Pirandello is no longer so frantic, so obsessively paternal about his daughter's affairs. He is more detached and reserved, and his frequent endearments are gone. He appeals more often to Lietta's own best judgment in deciding things as she thinks best. There is a sense that the atmosphere of oedipal relations that had existed between father and daughter for years had dissipated. The few letters from 1931 concern the practical matters of Lietta's return to Chile after a trip to Italy. Except for a brief meeting in 1933 in Buenos Aires, where Lietta met her father on the occasion of the world premiere of *When One Is Somebody*, the contacts between them were sporadic. All through these years relations between father and daughter also lacked the emotional intimacy they had had up until 1926.

There remain just three letters from 1936. Things have gotten bad in Chile, and Lietta is now intent on leaving Manuel, taking her children and returning to Italy. Pirandello writes to her at length about legal advice he has obtained for her, and what she must take care to do in legal terms before she rashly abandons her husband and takes their children away from him.

Constrained by the circumstances, Pirandello takes great pains to arrange for his daughter's trip to Italy and for her to be resettled in Rome. He offers to get her an apartment and have it furnished. In July, 1936, he writes her from Venice about what she should remember to bring:

> Between the trip and this furnishing [of an apartment] I will have to spend a not inconsiderable sum, and my financial situation is anything but flourishing. Therefore try to bring with you as much as you can, of house lines, of silver, of clothes for you and the children, to alleviate the expenses for me as much as possible (July 17, 1936, p. 121).

This was hardly an easy time for Pirandello. In October, 1935, on his return voyage from a two and a half month trip to the United States, he suffered a heart attack; two days later he had another more serious one. On the whole, the trip had not been highly successful; he had secured no contracts for movie adaptations of his plays, a failure that greatly disappointed him. Then, on September 10 of the next year, Marta left from Genoa on *The Conte di Savoia* bound for New York. As we know, Pirandello died at the end of that year, not long after Lietta had arrived, without a husband or means, to begin life again at her father's sole expense. Having arrived in Italy in October, Lietta spent afternoons with her father in his study, trying—now that Marta was gone—to recreate the harmony she had once had with her father. But she could also sense how far away his mind was—across the ocean with the woman who performed his plays. He seemed withdrawn and distant, as he had been during his years in Berlin or Paris. Moreover, from his letters it is clear that his financial means were stretched very thin, with three adult children dependent on him and living off his liberal support. Like Lietta, his sons had always depended on Pirandello's paternal generosity. And now the need to settle their father's estate came at precisely the moment when Lietta stood most in need.

The d'Amico Dynasty

Lietta's daughter Maria Luisa Aguirre—born just after her parent's return to Italy in 1925—married Alessandro d'Amico, son of the prominent theater critic Silvio d'Amico, the same critic who had often given Marta scathing reviews, and whom Marta and Pirandello called "that priest." With this marriage, Pirandello's descendants and heirs became part of one of the most powerful families in twentieth-century Italian arts and media. After Pirandello's death and the unexpected surfacing of his will, which awarded Marta the rights to nine plays, the old animosity toward the actress kicked into gear, resulting in a heated legal battle over the lucrative rights to Pirandello's literary patrimony. When Marta returned to Italy in the 1950s, she found herself in hostile country, and her enemies had become powerful in precisely the places that could hurt and hinder her the most—show business and criticism. It must be said that they did precisely that.

As we might predict of an influential art critic during Fascist times, Silvio d'Amico's projected critical authority could be authoritarian, and his strong prejudices were given free reign under the guise of being a more neutral arbiter of art and taste. His sons followed him into the arena of the literary intelligentsia; Fedele became a prominent musicologist, and Alessandro, like his father, a critic and historian of Italian theater. The d'Amico family became a veritable industry unto themselves in the twentieth-century world of journalistic criticism that was created by the growth of modern big media. Their considerable network of influences was tied to the power of media outlets—print, radio, television, cinema— and through this power they exercised influence over popular opinion and the careers of those who wished to be part of this world. Strong connections with the large publishing house Mondadori have served the d'Amico interests well over the years. Moreover, Fedele d'Amico was married to the famous screenwriter Suso Cecchi, the daughter of the art and film critic Emilio Cecchi, who was responsible for the (botched) screen adaptation of Pirandello's *Acciaio* and who Marta felt was responsible for her last-minute replacement from the film. This family relationship was yet another link in the chain that might obstruct Marta's access to work in Italy.

These family connections created the typical system of hereditary incumbency, in which being related to someone high-up provides a massive head start. In this situation it was easy to support family and friends, to exclude outsiders, and to thwart anyone who challenged their interests in any way. When the Italian journalist Oreste Del Buono famously dubbed them the "d'Amico clan" ("Non maltrattate i telefoni bianchi"), he touched a nerve, and Alessandro d'Amico reacted with venom. It was characteristic of the d'Amico family as a whole to respond vigorously whenever anybody made even the slightest criticism of anything touching their interests.

Alessandro d'Amico spent his career preserving the legacy of his father, cultivating his image, and continuing his work, especially on the *Enciclopedia dello Spettacolo*, with the addition of Pirandello to this project when he married Pirandello's granddaughter. In doing so Alessandro became the voice of both his father Silvio and of the Pirandello family as well. Alessandro used this privileged position to become the chief spokesman for Pirandello's legacy, with all the complexities this entailed. Pirandello's descendants have often had a vested interest in presenting him in an idealized light, and to downplay— even suppress—other aspects of his life and career less congenial to this ideal image. Marta Abba was caught squarely in the middle of this messy real-life drama involving the d'Amico and Pirandello families and their efforts to control the afterlife of Pirandello's works by crafting the 'proper' official memory of his life and career. Perhaps unsurprisingly, this sanitized version of Pirandello systematically, and as much as is feasible, excludes the presence of Marta Abba.

This marriage of one of the Pirandellos into the powerful d'Amico clan makes it easier to understand how it was possible for Maria Luisa Aguirre d'Amico to write and publish three books of reminiscence about her grandfather, each of them with introductory endorsements by important writers and critics like Leonardo Sciascia, Vincenzo Consolo, and Giovanni Macchia. In these memoirs she constructs a corrected image of Pirandello, with an editorial revision of history that is most egregious in taking every pain to avoid any mention of Marta Abba! It forces us to wonder why Marta, who played such an important and complex role in Pirandello's life for over a decade, would be scrubbed from the record of his life as it is presented by his family members.

The omission did not escape the notice of those who reviewed these books. The journalist Matteo Collura, for example, interviewed Maria Luisa Aguirre d'Amico when her *Vivere con Pirandello* came out, and was surprised that Marta Abba warranted no mention. Indeed, the author insisted when pressed that it was not her intention to write about Pirandello, but about her mother and grandmother. But this insistence seems to be a false pretense, since the Pirandello name, featuring prominently in the title, is the principal hook of interest for the book in the first place, and to insist that it is "not about Pirandello" is disingenuous. When pressed further about the glaring omission of Marta Abba, Maria Luisa repeated: "I have already said that I wanted to speak about my mother and grandmother. I did not intentionally choose not to name Abba." ("La dura vita delle signore Pirandello")

Still, when reading *Vivere con Pirandello,* those with some appreciation of the great importance of Marta Abba in Pirandello's last years cannot help but sense a certain forced silence on the matter. When the events compel it, Marta is referred to without being named. At the same time, the book contains curious ambiguities and a lack of details about Pirandello's strained relationship with his daughter Lietta, the author's mother. All in all, we cannot quite accept the author's claim that Marta's absence was not intentional. Nor does the generally hagiographic treatment of biographical and historical facts sit well with an academic public more intent on the truth than on shaping the case to particular interests and idealized images. On this point, finally, there is an interview with Andrea Pirandello (in *L'Unità* August 2, 1991), Stefano's son and thus Pirandello's grandson, in which he mentions that "one of the grandchildren, Lietta's daughter, has written about some of these family events, according to her own interpretation." The qualification is intriguing, and suggests that at the very least there may be other versions of the facts even within the Pirandello family.

Thus when Marta returned to Italy and the stage in the 1950s, the deck was stacked against her in the critical world. Her enemies chose to attack her by framing her as an 'old-fashioned' actress whose style was outdated. Like all good attacks, it was based partly on the truth. Marta's heyday had been with the Maestro. For her Pirandello's theater stood still in the 1920s and 1930s in a sort of frozen and haunting rendering that seemed to be from another time. The plays which had been so masterfully performed nearly thirty years before required an interpretation that progressed with the times. The mood of the theater had decisively changed. Moreover, the time in Italy when the theories of character immersion advanced by Stanislavsky had predominated as the preferred method was long past. It was not a coincidence that the actors of the Teatro d'Arte di Roma (named after the Moscow Art Theater founded in 1897 by Stanislavsky and Nemirovich-Danchenko) directed by Pirandello took the habit of writing the names of the characters they were to interpret in the evening on the doors of their respective dressing-rooms. Pirandello was certainly aware of the controversies surrounding the relationship of writer, director, actor and audience that had raged since the turn of the century. His theater aimed at aggravating them by exploring and exposing their assumptions and consequences.

Pirandello had adopted the method of absorption propounded by Stanislavsky on the basis of an aesthetic of the thorough interpenetration of art and life. In this method he selected as his protégée Marta Abba, who added to her performances in a magical frame that almost allowed her to suspend the characters the Maestro had written for her beyond space and time. The characters came to *belong* to Marta: "I am happy that my "Fulvia Gelli" (the female protagonist of *As Before, Better than Before*) also begins to become yours, if you tell me that you like her more and more. Also there, I believe, there is room to go deeper. And I am sure that nobody will ever be able to get more completely inside her than you do" (Rome, August 17, 1926; P, p. 9). Marta Abba remembered the events of that time clearly even after many years: "The Maestro wanted one to learn one's part by heart, with gusto, so that one actually *became* the character herself…he was tireless…" All this made her the most haunting and troubled actress of the neurotic theater of the time, which was still in its early stages. Every innovation that might have modified her 'approved' interpretation of the Maestro's roles, one sanctified in many cases by the success it had garnered in years past, seemed a betrayal both of the script and of the Maestro's own will. Not only did this feeling sway her, but, with the passage of years Marta Abba, ever more inclined to isolate herself in the abstract loneliness of her convictions, only took the role Pirandello had assigned her to extremes, gradually becoming not merely a devoted performer but the receptacle of absolute Pirandellian truths.

A Star is (Not Quite) Born

From the 1950s on, Marta's dramatic protests against various theatrical productions of Pirandello's works became common and infamous scenes, at times blocking the performance of those works to which she owned the rights. Among several especially memorable episodes was one recounted in vivid terms by the Italian actress Adriana Asti: "at the end of the fabulous Fifties, [Vittorio] Gassman [a famous Italian actor] called me and said: 'Do you want to play Mommina?' [the female lead in *Tonight we Improvise*]. So we opened at the Alfieri [Theater] in Turin, with a lot of anxiety, what am I saying, with complete chaos. The police came along, escorting the Abba sisters, magnificent custodians of the most intimate legacy of the Maestro" ("Mommina cara").

Convinced of her righteousness, and sure of being the sole repository of the Pirandellian Word, Marta Abba neglected any attempt to evolve, locking herself into an ever more stubborn silence, which she broke only on rare occasions. Nevertheless, there is some reason to be suspicious about this image of Marta Abba as being behind the times, old-fashioned, and fixed in old roles and styles when she returned to the theater in the 1950s. Indeed, it may well be an artifact of the hostile critical image constructed by the Pirandello-d'Amicos and others. For some who saw her perform in those days have very different memories. The well-known Italian writer and novelist Gina Lagorio, for instance, recalled in a 1994 newspaper article that she had seen Marta in 1954, in Florence, performing in *As You Desire Me*: "she was beautiful, very fine, her voice was more like an orchestra than a single instrument, subtle, profound, at times sharp and full, at other times even shrill." ("Passioni di Pirandello")

Marta was still, then, at least by some accounts, able to work magic on the stage in the 1950s. Yet as she grew older and changing fashions and tastes left her behind, the years of bitter struggle she waged to obtain and protect the copyrights the Maestro had bequeathed her in his will were not without their negative effects. Her enemies could be ruthless and cruel, and she became understandably somewhat guarded and taciturn in dealing with her interests, her public image, and the Pirandellian legacy she nurtured and sought to preserve.

Epilogue

THE LESS THAN AFFABLE GUARDIAN

After her divorce and return to Italy, Marta gradually took on the role of (in Giovanni Raboni's caustic phrase) the "less than affable guardian" of his letters, documents, and rights to a kind of exclusive 'Pirandelliana' over which she held sole authority. This book grew out of my reflections on Luigi Pirandello's correspondence and relationship with Marta Abba, as well as my own relationship with Marta in the course of research in the 1980s. I was supposed to edit the letters, but the privilege was taken from me suddenly and almost without explanation. The reason was to be found in the actress' bizarre and capricious personality. At the heart of this rupture were the letters, but also Marta's solitude and her desperate if unconscious clinging to life.

Marta Abba was 84 when I was in Milan doing research during a sabbatical year, and having been informed by Princeton that the actress wanted to leave the letters to the University, I knocked on her door. She greeted me like Norma Desmond in *Sunset Boulevard*—with the air of a great diva, and a way of doing things that was ostentatiously detached and 'divine.' After I gained her trust, Marta took me into her employment fulltime. Each day we would go to the bank where she kept Pirandello's letters in a safety deposit box, and there we would spend hours copying them. Back at her place, we would discuss them and organize the copies and the rest of the materials she had at home, which included her own letters to Pirandello. For her my own life meant nothing. I was there to work on the letters. I had to transcribe them, and to focus all my efforts exclusively on this. At times I had the bemused feeling that I was reliving a version of the drama that unfolds in Henry James' novella *The Aspern Papers*, though with the occasional fear that it might just come to the same dreadful end of the prized author's letters being burned.

My 'confinement,' as it were, by Marta Abba lasted from February to September, 1984. Her sister Cele was a constant companion in all our activities, whether taking a walk or going out to a restaurant. As the excitement of the nostalgia aroused by my work grew, Marta also suggested that I should take her and her sister to Sicily to revisit the places—such as *Caos*, the estate were Pirandello was born more than a century before—she had visited many years before with her Maestro. It was a fond idea, though we never did make the trip. The pitiful aspect of this sudden and unexpected new dependence on me that Marta developed, despite her queen-like demeanor (it ought to have been the other way around, since she had a new audience from which she could derive the intoxicating sensation of still being alive) exploded when my sabbatical was over and I returned to Princeton.

She called and wrote me relentlessly, expecting me to do the same in return. She always asked me about her and her sister coming to Princeton, for a very specific purpose. What she had in mind was to assemble a team of scholars at the university to compile a definitive edition of the letters under her direction. Privately I knew such a project was unlikely, and as it turned out the University was not forthcoming with an invitation. Marta took this somewhat badly, and, vastly overestimating my power to make such a decision, interpreted it as a result of my own reluctance.

And so when, busy as I was with teaching and other duties, my work on the letters gradually slowed, along with my calls and letters to her, she shut the door in my face. Feeling betrayed, she also banned me from continuing work on the letters and publishing the correspondence. In the spring of 1985, I searched for her in vain in Monte Carlo, hoping to explain that the work on the letters was done during my free time from my academic duties. She refused to see me. She also stopped writing to me. The parallel to Henry James' *Aspern Papers* came back to haunt me, and I feared the letters would now forever remain lost to posterity.

After long and tortuous negotiations, however, the following year the letters did arrive at Princeton University. Marta herself brought them, and a formal event was arranged for her to present her bequest before a public audience. (Sadly, I was not invited and did not attend.) This episode confirmed how terrible it can be for a once-great actress to be on 'sunset boulevard.' Her performance (as other relayed it to me) was a dramatic monologue, in the spirit of Ilse from *The Mountain Giants* who says at the end of the unfinished masterpiece's second act: "That means I shall proceed alone to read the *Tale*, if I shall be unable to perform it." The letter she chose to read from pictured Pirandello as the insomniac writer, the restless martyr to art and imagination, the romantic philosophical soul pained to his very depths by the impression of a sunrise:

> I kept on working through the night. At 3:00 I began to see at the two windows of my study the first transparency of dawn, like a mystery that was attempting to disclose itself from far, far away, uncertain whether the side of the huge Lutzow Square appeared like profiles of mountains against that first shimmer, and I had—I do not know how remote, that appeared through the glass of a train window while I was traveling, and far away on the horizon was seen, still black, a range of hills. A feeling of mysterious and most profound pain. Pain of all life condemned every day to reawaken from the forgetful sleep of night. The benefit of sleep was denied me tonight, and the journey…wasn't my life one long journey without arrivals, without rest? Seated in front of my writing desk in an alien house, far away, here I am, without a home of my own upon this earth anymore, deprived of my own bed in which to sleep…and the dawn, as from the glass window of the train that had been running all night, surprised me tonight from the windowpanes of my study, sleepless, as it did then. Will the work I have done ever compensate for the pain that this dawn has given me, as I drown the bitterness of my individual fate in the universal bitterness of this most useless mortal life? (Berlin, May 24, 1930; P, pp. 142-3).

With the gift of the correspondence to Princeton University, the United States again became a land of dreams, assuring the actress a kind of sacred custodianship over material of great general, and not merely personal, cultural value, under the aegis of a prestigious institution far removed from controversies and acrimonious debates. The material was thus removed, in Marta's words, from the "sight of the indiscrete" of those who "just didn't understand."

At the age of 86 and now moving only with difficulty, Marta Abba once again had an audience that was invited to celebrate her, or better yet, to form a suitable backdrop for her. The mood was festive but solemn, as though a rite involving a goddess was on the verge of being consummated. The atmosphere remained heavily theatrical. Aware that she was performing her last role, Marta Abba read a few of the most memorable passages chosen from the letters Pirandello wrote her in some of his most trying moments, intoning them with her deep and unmistakable timbre. Her voice, her words, her pauses—all brought back to life the torments, disillusions, and worries of the man who, alone and poignantly, wrote to her from Germany during the years of their close friendship. But the implicit confession of the dimensions of her professional relationship with Pirandello also conjured up the unexpected onset of love, which had been couched in mystery for more than half a century.

Modulating skillfully, as both her life and her art had taught her, during the last scene of her last act in Princeton, Marta Abba read some selections from among the most moving of the letters as if from a play written solely for her, in which the Maestro expresses all his feelings "of mysterious and most profound pain. Pain of all life condemned every day to reawaken from the forgetful sleep of night." Feelings and powerful emotions sealed into the letters which Marta Abba, in a gesture made despite her conflicting feelings, wished to hand over to this country, where Pirandello had often dreamed of realizing his fortunes in wealth, life, and love, together with her.

Marta lived until June 24, 1988. Becoming ever more inaccessible to the very end, she died like a goddess—who cannot, and must not, transform herself into any woman, or open up her own temple to indiscrete gazes, leaving behind the passions and hatreds that had passed through her and of which she had been made the object.

WORKS CITED

Abba, Marta. *Caro Maestro… Lettere a Luigi Pirandello 1926-1936*. Ed. Pietro Frassica. Milan: Mursia, 1994.

Aguirre D'Amico, Maria Luisa. *Vivere con Pirandello*. Milan: Mondadori, 1989.

Alvaro, Corrado. Preface, *Novelle per un anno*. Milan: Mondadori, 1956. 33-4.

Asti, Adriana. "Mommina cara." *L'espresso*, July 6, 1988.

Barthes, Roland. *Mythologies*. New York: Hill and Wang, 1972.

Cecchi, Emilio. "Luigi Pirandello pittore." *Almanacco Letterario Bompiani*. Milan, 1938.

Matteo Collura. "La dura vita delle signore Pirandello", *Corriere della sera*, November 19, 1989.

D'Amico, Alessandro, and Alessandro Tinterri, eds. *Pirandello capocomico*. Palermo: Sellerio, 1987.

Del Buono, Oreste. "Telefoni bianchi e premi leghisti." *La stampa. Tuttolibri*, February 1994.

Frassica, Pietro. *A Marta Abba per non morire*. Milan: Mursia, 1991.

Freud, Sigmund. "Three Essays on Sexuality." *Complete Psychological Works of Sigmund Freud*. Ed. J. Strachey. London: Hogarth Press/Institute of Psychoanalysis, 1953. 74-77.

Gardair, Jean-Michel. "Il gioco delle parti: Maschile e femminile." *La Persona nell'opera di Luigi Pirandello*. Milan: Mursia, 1990. 111-19.

Lagorio Gina, "Passioni di Pirandello", *L'Unità*, May 16, 1994.

Ludwig, Emil. *Talks with Mussolini*. Boston: Little, Brown, and Company, 1933.

Masino, Paola. "Pirandello e il *Corriere*, 1876-1986." Special insert, *Corriere della Sera*, May 28 1986.

Mussolini, Benito. *Scritti e discorsi*. Milan: Hoepli, 1934.

Nardelli, Federico Vittore. *L'uomo segreto. Vita e croci di Luigi Pirandello*. Milan: Mondadori, 1932.

Pirandello, Andrea. *Pirandello. L'uomo lo scrittore il teatrante*. Milan: Mazzotta, 1987.

Pirandello, Luigi. *Album di famiglia di Luigi Pirandello*. Ed. Maria Luisa Aguirre D'Amico. Palermo: Sellerio, 1979.

—-. *Her Husband*, Durham and London: Duke University Press, 2000.

—-. "In America la vita è dei vivi." *Corriere della Sera*, June 16th, 1929.

—-. *Lettere a Lietta*. Ed. Maria Luisa Aguirre D'Amico. Milan: Mondadori, 1999.

—-. *Lettere a Marta Abba*. Ed. Benito Ortolani. Milan: Mondadori, 1995.

—-. *Novelle per un anno*. Pref. by Corrado Alvaro. Milan: Mondadori, 1969.

—-. *Pirandello's Love Letters to Marta Abba*. Ed. Benito Ortolani. Princeton: Princeton University Press, 1994.

—-. *Saggi, poesie, scritti varii*. Ed. Manlio Lo Vecchio-Musti. Milan: Mondadori, 1973.

—-. *The Notebooks of Serafino Gubbio, or, Shoot!* Trans. C.K. Scott Moncrieff. Sawtry: Dedalus, 1990.

Raboni, Giovanni. "Esce di scena Marta Abba, la favorita di Pirandello." *Corriere della Sera*, June 26, 1988.

Venturi, A. "Pirandello oltre la maschera; un pittore conformista." *La Stampa* (Tuttolibri), July 12, 1984.

Vittori, Rossano. *Il trattamento cinematografico dei "Sei personaggi" testo inedito di Luigi Pirandello*. Florence: Liberoscambio, 1984.

Breinigsville, PA USA
06 November 2010
248778BV00002B/1/P